Continuous Excursions

Marshall Colman

Continuous Excursions
Politics and Personal Life

Pluto Press

First published in Great Britain by
Pluto Press Limited, Unit 10 Spencer Court,
7 Chalcot Road, London NW1 8LH

Copyright © Marshall Colman 1982

ISBN 0 86104 357 X

Cover designed by Clive Challis
Cover photograph by Mark Rusher

Typeset by Grassroots Typeset, London NW6.
Printed in Great Britain by Photobooks (Bristol) Limited,
28 Midland Road, Bristol

Contents

Preface

Most political thinkers take it for granted that politics and personal life are quite separate from one another, assuming that politics is restricted to the major issues that affect nations, and that personal life is restricted to the daily affairs of individuals. They admit that affairs of state and personal affairs may impinge on one another — no-one would deny, for example, that taxation affects individuals or that the character of a leader can affect the actions of a government — but nobody in the past has come anywhere near saying what modern feminists say: that the personal *is* political.

The women's movement stands out from all other political movements (with the possible exceptions of anarchism and utopian socialism) in that it seeks not merely a particular change in government policies, or a revolution against the existing political system, but a transformation in the nature of politics itself. Feminists aspire to a type of politics in which major issues will become a part of everyday life and everyday life will become a major political issue — they aspire to a *personal politics* which will politicise every aspect of our lives, including intimate personal relations.

Because the personal and the political have been forced apart everyone thinks they are separate. So, for advocates of personal politics, ways must be found of bringing them together out of their unnatural isolation. Those advocates of personal politics who belong to political organisations refuse to let the organisation dominate their lives, and insist that their private life is as important as the time they spend at meetings; they make sure that women's issues are discussed in their parties and unions; they strive to bring their personal relations into line with their political principles; and they scrutinise their actions and thoughts to root out anything ideologically doubtful.

Practical difficulties arise when one tries to apply the principles of personal politics. How much of the agenda of a political meeting, for instance, should personal matters take up? If they are just as important as the big impersonal issues, should they be permitted to push them out entirely? How far should the scrutiny of personal relations go? Should we analyse every attitude and action even if it seems relatively harmless? To what extent should feminists and socialists make the external details of their lives conform to their political ideals? Does it matter if they become eccentric and cliquey as a result?

There are theoretical as well as practical difficulties, and the practical difficulties are not made any easier by theoretical confusion. In the first flush of enthusiasm for personal politics some people believed that all distinctions between the personal and the political should be removed. They lived in communes where everything was shared, they renounced monogamy, and they abandoned privacy. Almost without exception these experiments ended in unhappiness, and now few people think this is the right way to live. But the idea that you can fuse the personal and the political lives on. The practical and theoretical difficulties arise because no-one has really explained what it *means* to say that the personal is political or that the personal and the political can be fused. If we could understand what the relation between politics and personal life is we could avoid intellectual confusion and practical disaster. My aim in writing this book has been to clarify that relation.

I begin by describing how the personal politics movement emerged, then I say what politics and personal life are and consider social relations, sexual relations and personal relations, saying how each can be political. I distinguish various kinds of personal relations, ranging from the most intense to the most casual kind. Casual relations in public — the relations between strangers — are not often regarded as personal at all, because we think all personal relations are intimate, but I argue that non-intimate relations are just as personal as intimate ones and that public events are just as much a part of life as private ones. I go on to consider the accusation that personal politics is individualistic. I also say something about the history of personal life, for there is an argument that personal life is a recent innovation which only came into being with modern capitalism.

Even though personal life is not new its character has changed, and one of the most important changes has been a decrease in the vitality of public life. By this I mean that non-intimate personal relations have become fewer and more perfunctory. By constrast, intimate relations in private have assumed an undue importance. I say why personal politics ought to concern itself more with relations in public and less with relations in private. By concerning itself so much with private relations it simply carries on the process that has devitalised public life, whereas personal politics should also be about the revitalisation of public life.

I owe a debt of gratitude to the women's movement for opening up this area of personal politics. My own experiences of traditional politics have been similar to those of many women: the toughness, combativeness and maleness of politics have always put me off and personal politics has felt like a breath of fresh air in the stifling corridors of the left. The opportunity to reconcile politics and personal life is a thing I welcome with enthusiasm. In the past it always seemed that one was forced to make a choice between politics, which was personally unsatisfying but effective, and personal life, which was satisfying but politically ineffective. Now there is some prospect of combining the two.

There is one point of style I need to explain. I tend to use 'she' rather than 'he' as the universal pronoun, and in most contexts 'she' refers to both women and men. This seems to me the most satisfactory solution to the problem of the pronoun, and, what is more, gives a slight shock to our sexist assumptions.

Many people have helped me with this book. Dave Harker and Alistair McGechie both discussed early drafts with me and I have benefited greatly from their continued interest. Catherine Athill, Stan Cohen, Marcelle Rudolph, Brian Taylor and Chris Wilson have also read the manuscript and have made useful suggestions. Audrey Summerhill's enthusiasm at an early stage encouraged me greatly. Other people have given me ideas in the course of our conversations, some of them without realising it, and of these I should like to single out Bernard Brown, Warren Colman, Frances Gorman, Ros Kane, Jeff Rudin and Martin Yarnit. Chris Draper, Gary Ewer, Chris Havell, John Keefe and Simon Macdonald helped me clarify my thoughts by discussing Chapter 6 with me in our men's group. In Chapter 7 I have drawn on the ideas in Stephen Lukes's *Individualism*, in Chapter 10 on Richard Sennett's *The Fall of Public Man* and in Chapter

11 on Hannah Arendt's *The Human Condition*. I should also like to acknowledge the support I have received from Ann Colman, Gerald Colman, Florence Hamilton, Mary Igoe and Ken Ward. Finally I should like to thank Richard Kuper and Peter Ayrton at Pluto Press for their painstaking work on the manuscript and Behjat Reziah for typing it.

1.   The Personal is Political

On an autumn evening in 1911 hundreds of suffragettes walked determinedly out of a meeting at Caxton Hall in London, went to Whitehall, and broke as many windows as they could. Two hundred and twenty-three women were arrested that night. The following March, late one afternoon, when the West End was at its busiest, respectable women suddenly produced stones from their muffs and smashed window panes all the way along Piccadilly. Soon the peace was shattered again as the sound of breaking glass was heard in Regent Street. Fifteen minutes later another wave broke over Oxford Street as a third battalion broke windows there. 'From every part of the crowded and brilliantly-lit streets came the crash of splintered glass,' wrote a *Daily Mail* reporter. 'People started as a window shattered at their side; suddenly there was another crash in front of them; on the other side of the street; behind — everywhere. Scared shop assistants came running out to the pavements; traffic stopped; policemen sprang this way and that; five minutes later the streets were a procession of excited groups, each surrounding a woman wrecker being led in custody to the nearest police station.'[1]

These demonstrations marked the renewal of a militant campaign by the Women's Social and Political Union, a campaign that was to last until the outbreak of war when the 'women's army', as Mrs Pankhurst called it, declared a truce in its war with the government. In those few years politicians all over the country were heckled, harassed, horsewhipped and stoned; GPO letter-boxes were set on fire; priceless paintings were slashed; cabinet ministers' golf-courses were dug up; buildings were vandalised, razed to the ground and blown sky high. In their determination to get the vote and to be admitted to political life on equal terms with men, these women mounted a campaign more militant, and created in the capital an atmosphere more tense and fearful, than anything experienced in Britain since.

When women finally got the vote, it seemed they had at last won the place in political life they deserved. Once they gained the franchise the majority of feminists were convinced that they could now use politics for the improvement of employment, education, family law, and women's rights. Mrs Pankhurst was adopted as a parliamentary candidate, Nancy Astor became the first woman to sit in the Commons, and the militancy of the women's movement died away.

But the women's movement of the seventies raised once again the question that many thought the vote had settled: What is women's relation to politics? This movement was different. Whereas English suffragism had emerged from the Liberal and Labour parties, the new American feminism grew out of the radical, left, and black-power movements. The issues it concerned itself with were broader, and its analysis of women's disabilities went deeper. It saw its task not as that of getting emancipation by means of administrative reforms, but of liberating women in the depth of their personal lives. Politics took on a new aspect. Feminists realised that the issues which had traditionally been the only ones fit for politics — international relations, housing, employment, education, and so on — did not exhaust the range of political issues. Women's relations with men, their confinement to the home, their role in childbearing and childcare, their sexual feelings, the very control of their own bodies — these were all thrust into the political arena. New expressions bore witness to this new conception of politics: 'the politics of the family', 'sexual politics', and 'the politics of experience'.

Hysteria — supposedly a female condition — was the first response of many men to this redefinition of politics, and, surprisingly enough, some of the most hysterical responses came from socialist men. When, at a conference of Students for a Democratic Society, in the United States, black-power delegates demanded that blacks have half the votes, the men all nodded. When a woman demanded that women have half the votes, the men all laughed.[2] While the women's liberation movement was still finding its feet women decided to speak for women at an anti-Nixon rally in Washington in 1969. They wanted not to attack or to hector, simply to make the point that voting could do nothing to help women out of their particular oppression. The men burst into cat-calls, boos and guffaws. They silenced women with shouts of, 'Take it off! Take her off and fuck her!'[3]

This was not to be a unique event; women have suffered similar reactions time and time again in the intervening years.

When men respond to feminism in this way they do more than exclude women from politics. They exclude from politics matters that, in their view, have nothing to do with politics at all. The family, housework, childbearing, sexuality, intimate relations, feelings and desires — the things that women concern themselves with — are, according to these traditional socialists, purely personal matters. Politics is one thing, personal life another.

Personal politics

Feminists reacted to this tearing apart of politics and personal life by declaring that the personal *is* political, and in doing so they created a challenging slogan now heard beyond the confines of the women's movement. By means of it they have made us realise several things about politics and personal life.

The first is that politics should be more relevant to our private lives. Personal matters should not be relegated from the conference chamber to the bedchamber. We should change politics so that it touches us more closely, and so that people's immediate concerns are not lost from view when policies are adopted. Socialism is not enough, for even in a socialist society politics can be organised in such a way that the big issues always force out the little ones. Even a socialist Minister for the Family might not do the washing up.

The second thing feminists have made us realise is that personal life is not only relevant to politics, but that it is *in itself* political. Politics is about power, and power exists in the relations between individuals as well as in the state and the public sphere. Whether these relations are freely chosen (as in the case of friends) or not (as in the case of worker and boss) power is exerted in them to some degree.

And the third is that an authoritarian society depends not just on a particular structure or on particular institutions, but on a particular type of relationship between the individuals in it.

In drawing attention to these three things the women's movement has created something new: personal politics. Personal politics means making politics more relevant to personal life, struggling for growth and freedom in one's personal relations, and changing the personal relations that maintain authoritarian social structures. Personal politics is not entirely new: there is a long tradition of feminism, anarchism and utopian socialism in which the personal side of politics has been recognised. But the women's movement gave personal politics a new lease of life and brought together matters that were previously unconnected.

Personal politics has several sources. The black freedom movements of the sixties gave a great deal of attention to the experience of oppression. The hippy movement, with its advocacy of alternative life-styles and altered consciousness, was also an influence. The hippies had no time for the left with its organisations and discipline. It was to them a part of the straight society that made war and conditioned everybody to boredom. Through drugs and meditation, rock music and sensuality they created a kind of politics rooted in individual experience. Laing and Marcuse, the gurus of the new left, provided theoretical ammunition for the politics of consciousness. Laing coined the phrase 'the politics of experience', and in his explanations of the schizophrenic experience he insisted that unusual ways of seeing the world should not be suppressed. Marcuse argued that consciousness was of considerable political importance, and his analysis of advanced industrial capitalism concentrated on the deformation of individuality caused by the system. Black power, the hippies and the new left were all part of an amorphous movement that seemed set fair to sweep away traditional politics and to transform society by means of acid trips, open air rock concerts, going mad and getting laid.

Women's liberation inherited from this movement its emphasis on the personal and subjective, and it has had in turn exerted a beneficial influence on the socialist movement. Even those socialists who still reject feminism can no longer afford to ignore it. As galling to feminists as ritual genuflections to women's issues may be, they show that women's liberation is now a force to be reckoned with. Some feminists despair of getting personal politics taken really seriously in male-dominated organisations, but others are struggling slowly and by no means unsuccessfully to get it on to the agenda of socialist groups. And there are some men who are eager to take these matters up, having themselves felt dissatisfied with a socialism that is so external to their lives and so restricted in its concerns.

Fusing the personal and the political

Personal politics began as women's gut reaction to the treatment
they had experienced at the hands of traditional leftists. They
had sat silent in meetings while men did all the talking. They had
made the coffee while men did the 'important' work. They had
stayed at home looking after the children while men engaged in
the 'real' business of political life. In the new left and the civil
rights movement, where men had campaigned for the freedom
of blacks and Vietnamese, women found that *they* had no
freedom, and that *they* were victims of male imperialism. It was
time to bring politics home

What began as a gut reaction matured into a theory.
Feminists developed an analysis of male domination which
showed a connection between the personal and the political. In
the last twelve years many books and articles on personal politics
have appeared, some of them rooted in women's personal experience, some of them abstract and theoretical. Just as 'the
personal is political' was taken up outside the women's movement, so the theoretical issues of personal politics have been
taken up by men as well.

Some of the theory of personal politics is simplistic. I think
its oversimplifications correspond to the experiments in personal
life that people made in the early seventies. They made them not
only in reaction against traditional left politics, but also in the
wake of the events of 1968, which seemed to herald widespread
social changes but whose achievements were so much smaller
than everyone's expectations. The May Days in Paris, and the
tremor they sent round the world, were followed by retrench-
ment. The seventies saw the beginning of a capitalist slump and
the growth of the strong state. Libertarian experiments in life
styles were made partly in retreat, partly out of an enthusiasm
for personal politics. There was confidence about the right way
to live and a boldness, even a recklessness, in the relationships
people formed. This boldness reflected itself in the theories of
personal politics that evolved at that time, and although today
people are less confident that life-style experiments are a
panacea, many oversimplifications remain.

Personal politics began by insisting on making connections
between politics and personal life, but its meaning gradually
changed. People began to speak not so much of the *connection*

between the personal and the political as of their *unity* or *fusion*. They ceased to regard them as two separate things that are linked, and began to regard them as the same thing. The fusion of the personal and the political has become the main idea of personal politics. 'The politics of experience *fuses* the personal and the political,' wrote Juliet Mitchell,[4] and this idea has been echoed in many discussions about politics and personal life. Reacting against the rigid separation between the personal and the political that prevails in traditional politics, people developed an enthusiasm for eliminating distinctions in their lives. Personal politics saw how the nuclear family separated women from the wider society and the home from work; so women tried to live in a way that not only overcame their isolation, but also brought home and work closer together. It saw the difference in quality between personal relations in private, which are warm, intimate and expressive, and those in public, which are distant, formal and inimical to self-expression; so people tried to transform personal relations in a way that made them all intimate and expressive. It saw that sexual monogamy made couples inward looking, and non-sexual friendships unimportant; so people attacked romantic love and said sexual relationships ought not to have a special status. It saw the way that the cultivation of individuality is linked with competitive individualism; so people discouraged the separation of what is individual from what is collective. Personal politics has come to say that we should overcome distinctions and separations — between personal and political, private and public, intimate and formal, individual and collective, house and work, friend and lover. That everything is political, that everything is connected, and that we should not separate one thing from another — these are ideas that have come to be commonly expressed in the personal politics movement.

Some socialists committed to personal politics have adopted a similar view. They have said that although separations are unavoidable at the moment they will disappear in a socialist society, because they are created by capitalism and cannot last without it. This means, they say, that the fight for socialism and women's liberation obliges us to fight for the unity of the personal and the political. As one writer puts it, 'Until we can get over the division of the world into two spheres — one emotional and personal and female, the other aggressive and impersonal and male — we are simply aiding and abetting the continuation of capitalist patriarchy.'[5] Eli Zaretsky advances a similar argument in *Capitalism, the Family and Personal Life*. The personal, he says, came into being with capitalism, before which there was no division between home and work or personal and political. When capitalism goes, these divisions will go as well.

The idea of fusing the personal and the political is by no means unambiguous. On the one hand, it is interpreted to mean that, since everything personal is political, you do not have to do anything in particular to be political. Since personal relations are just as political as international relations, no-one can say that concentrating all your energies on personal relations is less political than taking an interest in foreign affairs. On the other hand it is interpreted to mean that, since there should be no division of our lives into a 'personal' part and a 'political' part, there is nothing personally damaging in devoting all our energies to political activities. The idea of fusing the personal and the political leads to a lack of balance because striking a balance between politics and personal life requires us to recognise that they cannot be fused. So we find in the personal politics movement these two extreme views — one excessively personal, the other excessively political.

The excessively personal interpretation effectively collapses politics into personal life. People look inwards, concentrating on their personal experiences to the exclusion of social and public activity. The important forms of political activity become things that centre round one's personal life — things like consciousness-raising, food co-ops and babysitting rotas. All these things are important, and the great virtue of personal politics is that it has shown that they are important. But if we ignore the objective class structure of society, we end up with a one-sided and excessively personal view of politics.

On the other hand, the excessively political interpretation of personal politics effectively collapses personal life into politics. I can best explain this with the example of a friend who had a job as a community worker in an inner-city area. He was fortunate in that he was not confined to a nine-to-five existence, and he did a lot of his work in the evenings. He went to innumerable meetings and spent a lot of his time forming caucuses and alliances far into the night, huddled in a pub and arguing till closing time. After two years of frantic activity he persuaded himself that he had successfully fused the personal with the political. There was no hard-and-fast line between his work and his politics, his job and his home-life, those who were colleagues and those who were friends. But as this hectic activity began to take its toll he realised that he had not really fused the personal and political at all. All that had happened was that he had stopped going home. He had given up his personal life, and he had done so not because of the pressures of work but because he felt *guilty* about having a personal life. You can see the same pattern in the lives of many politically dedicated people, and the disease is by no means confined to the left. MPs and councillors of all parties have the same experience, staying at meetings till all hours and neglecting their personal lives. But only in certain left circles is such self-flagellation graced with the description 'fusing the personal and the political'. Most people call it 'overwork'.

The excessively political interpretation of personal politics takes another form as well. Here it is not a question of denying one's needs, but of thinking about everything in abstract terms. Take a man I knew who had decided to make important changes in his personal life and who was called upon to explain himself. Until then he had owned his own house, but now the time had come when he wanted to sell the house and move into his lover's shared household. His father — middle-class and middle-aged — could not understand this behaviour. 'Tell me,' he said, 'why do you choose to sell your house? Why do you not marry this woman if you love her? Why do you want to share everything with these people?' The father genuinely wanted to understand, and the son genuinely wanted to make him understand. His reply, however, consisted of a lengthy analysis of patriarchy and capitalism and of the need for new structures if one wanted to break with oppressive social systems. It is as if he missed the meaning of his own wishes and preferences and needed to find a political motive for everything he did. But there are more immediate causes of our actions than world-historical systems and the interplay between them — causes closer to the home and to the heart, and it is not always necessary to refer to anything other than these when someone asks us, 'Why do you want to do this?' The habit some people have got into, of explaining their personal lives in political and social terms, shows them to be dead to their feelings, and the odd thing is that some people committed to personal politics should also sometimes show this emotional anaesthesia.

From the margin to the centre

A remarkable pamphlet was published recently called *My Sex Life*. Its author, Chris Knight, described with exceptional frankness his relationship with Ann Bliss, with whom he had lived for several years. It was a brave attempt to publicise their personal life and to discover the political content of their intimate relations. Chris came to the conclusion that marriage doesn't work, especially for women, because it isolates and oppresses them, and that it doesn't work for men either, for even in successful marriages both parties 'delude themselves unendingly for the sake of the relationship'. After some years with him Ann decided that the relationship restricted her too much and that he was too possessive. Determined to break out, she slept with other men. Chris had been theoretically convinced of the correctness of feminism, but Ann now forced him to accept its practical implications for the first time. He relinquished his hold over her, renounced his need for monogamy, and became a house-husband.

Both Chris and Ann rejected delusion and self-sacrifice in principle and learned to see their relationship in a political light. But in the end Chris got the relationship between the personal and the political wrong because his account of his marriage is too political and too abstract. Here was a genuine conflict of needs: Chris had a need for a stable relationship, Ann had a need for a freer life. The marriage was a denial of Ann's needs, but a fulfilment of Chris's. Ending the marriage was a denial of Chris's needs but a fulfilment of Ann's. The conflict cannot be explained in any other way. Chris's desire for monogamy, his fidelity, his willingness to share housework and his readiness to look after the children cannot be described as sexist, and so one cannot invoke patriarchy to explain the conflict.

'All of us have to suffer to become revolutionaries,' he says. 'In my case the suffering was primarily sexual.'[6] My reaction on reading a statement like this is to wonder why we should suffer to become revolutionaries? If personal politics makes demands of this sort, how can it ever hope to have any widespread influence? If we tell people they have to suffer they will reply, perfectly reasonably, that they have suffered quite enough and that if personal politics means they are going to suffer even more then they are not interested. 'To get socialism we've got to put needs — our needs — first,' writes Ann in her version of the events Chris describes.[7] Putting our needs first seems far more sensible than suffering for politics.

The personal politics movement is a curious mixture of accepting people and making impossible demands of them, recognising human weakness and requiring superhuman strength, telling people to trust their own feelings and emphasising ideological correctness. If it ends up creating an elite of morally pure individuals it will have betrayed its original promise — to broaden the meaning of politics so that it touches ordinary people more closely, and, in particular to widen the appeal of socialism so that is no longer an affair of tiny meetings in smoke-filled rooms. If personal politics becomes so demanding that only a small number of people can cope with it it will move closer towards the margins of political life and will leave the majority untouched.

One of the reasons socialism has failed to appeal to those it hopes to appeal to is that it has failed to make the connections between politics and the personal. It has remained abstract and has taken little account of everyday concerns. Most people are preoccupied with their personal lives, and quite justifiably so. Politics seems to be far-removed from them, and over-concerned with big and impersonal issues. In the 1930s Wilhelm Reich criticised the German Communist Party for ignoring the needs of the masses and the sexual misery they suffered. When he opened his first Sex-Pol clinic in Berlin his views were vindicated by the tens of thousands of ordinary people who flocked there. He warned the Party that it was headed for disaster because it would not make the connection between personal life and socialism. His worst fears were realised when he saw not only the triumph of Hitler, but also the defection of working-class communists to a Nazi Party that paid more attention to their unconscious longings than did the communist movement.

We cannot get the balance right if we continue to talk about 'fusing the personal and the political' or 'uniting' them, or 'overcoming the split' between them. This just leads to confusion. If we are to get it right we have to be clear first of all what we mean by the personal and the political. What *are* personal relations, and how do they differ from social relations? What *is* sexual politics, and is it any different from politics in the traditional sense? What *is* public life, and how do we distinguish it from private life? I want to sort out some of these problems and confusions in the following chapters, and although I do not pretend to deal with them systematically, I hope to clarify what it means to say 'the personal is political'. As we shall see, the slogan conceals as much as it reveals.

2. Social Relations and Politics

It is not easy to say how the social differs from the personal. 'Social' and 'personal' are not even clearly differentiated in the English language. For example, we say that a person does not have much of a social life when we mean that her personal relations do not amount to much, and we say that someone is anti-social when we mean that she is not much given to friendship. Since 'social' sometimes *means* personal, it may seem academic to insist that social relations are different from personal ones. But it is not an academic distinction, for on it depends the style of politics we create.

There are, after all, usages of 'social' that refer to something very different from personal life. For example, the declining profitability of capital is clearly a social event. So is a rise in the rate of unemployment, the outbreak of war, or the increase of lead pollution in the atmosphere. Movements and trends like this are large and impersonal — clearly different from the 'social life' that consists of going out with friends or visiting the family.

Social relations

Social relations are impersonal in the sense that they do not necessarily involve face-to-face contact between individuals. The simplest type are the ones that individuals form in order to get their livelihood. In primitive societies people form bands for the purpose of hunting. This is a social relation where all the individuals meet together. But even in primitive societies there are other forms of social relations; for example, complicated rules of marriage and kinship in accordance with which clans and tribes enter into relations with one another, in the course of which gifts and dowries are often made. In these relations we can see the germ of the sort of relation on which many individuals, who do not ever meet one another, depend for their livelihood. In medieval Europe, people got most of the things they needed from a small number of people living close by them, but although lords and nobles got their basic requirements from their manors, they got their luxuries — gold and spices, oranges and silk — from overseas. In the course of the trade in luxuries, individuals who lived thousands of miles apart, and who did not know of each other's existence, were brought into relation with each other. Capitalism, which is based on trade and exchange, has made relations of this kind very extensive.

One of the most vivid pictures of this connection and mutual depedency was drawn by Adam Smith in his description of the invisible bond between a labourer and countless others.

> The woollen coat which covers the day-labourer, as coarse and rough as it may appear, is the product of the joint-labour of a great multitude of workmen. The shepherd, the sorter of wool, the wool-comber, the carder, the dyer, the scribbler, the spinner, the weaver, the fuller, the dresser, with many others, must all join their different arts in order to complete even this homely production. How many merchants and carriers besides, must have been employed in transporting the materials from some of those workmen to others who live in very distant parts of the country! How much commerce and navigation in particular, how many ship-builders, sailors, sail-makers, rope-makers, must have been employed in order to bring together the different drugs made use of by the dyer, which often come from the remotest corners of the world! What a variety of labour too is necessary in order to produce the tools of the meanest of those workmen. To say nothing of such complicated machines as the ship of the sailor, the mill of the fuller, or even the loom of the weaver, let us consider only what a variety of labour is requisite in order to form that very simple machine, the shears with which the shepherd clips the wool. The miner, the builder of the furnace for smelting the ore, the feller of the timber, the burner of the charcoal to be made use of in the smelting-house, the brick-maker, the workmen who attend the furnace, the mill-wright, the forger, the smith, must all of them join their different arts in order to produce them.[1]

Adam Smith was writing in the 1770s and was describing production of a relatively simple kind. Most of the materials he mentions were produced in Britain and the machinery he describes was unsophisticated. Nowadays every national economy depends more on imports, and industrial methods of production are extremely complex. The web of mutual dependency is more fine-meshed than it was two hundred years ago. This fact is driven home every time there is any interruption in manufacture in one part of industry and another part grinds to a halt. For example, an explosion in the ICI chemical plant at Billington on Teeside was followed nine months later by workers at a synthetic fibre factory in Cornwall being laid off. The workers in Cornwall probably did not know the workers at Billington, but there was a relation between them nonetheless. Events of this kind show that social relations, unlike personal relations, do not necessarily involve any face-to-face contact between people. Personal relations, on the other hand, cannot exist without face-to-face contact.

Another difference between personal and social relations is that, whereas the former are relations between individuals, the latter are relations between groups. The relation between Smith's labourer and the charcoal burner was not a pure type of social relation. They may have had no direct contact, but they had indirect contact through the tailor, the merchant, the shepherd, and so on. The pure type of social relation cannot be described in this way, because it does not consist of individuals at all.

The relationship between the town and the country is also a social relation although many people do not recognise this. Influenced by the romantic outlook, they see town and country as utterly different and unconnected. In the countryside resides all that is peaceful and virtuous, in the town all that is turbulent and vicious. But there has always been a relation between town and country. Even the virtues of one are linked with the vices of the other.

Although we often think of the countryside as 'nature', it is not at all natural. It is more a produce of artifice than nature. If it were not for human industry, England would be nothing but a forest. At times the English countryside has been shaped more by the *idea* of nature than by nature itself. The landscapes that surround the great country houses are often produced by great labours of earth-moving. In the eighteenth and early nineteenth centuries men like Humphrey Repton and Capability Brown designed these landscapes and called for massive alterations in what had been before. Trees were uprooted because they spoiled the view. Woods were planted because they improved it. Rivers were diverted. Unsightly cottages and offensive villages were razed. Farmers were driven from their holdings to make a grand expanse of park.

As manufacturing industry developed, the wealth of country estates was drawn more and more from the towns, landowners investing in factories and gradually depending less upon agricultural production. At the same time the difference between the appearance of the countryside and the appearance of the towns grew more marked, and the closer the relation between town and country became the more different they looked. In some instances the very slums which marred the town were owned by proprietors of the estates that contrasted so sharply with them.

This contrast grew out of a relation between landed aristocrats and urban paupers. It was by no means a personal relation, and was mediated by cash. It was a relation between two groups, the members of which had no contact with one another, and this is the essence of all class relations.

It is not always easy to see this, because members of different classes do sometimes come into contact with one another. In the countryside, landowners and their employees do so fairly frequently, both inside and outside work. In the town there are fewer personal contacts between members of different classes, but they exist nonetheless. The executive and the typist may happen to bump into each other in the pub. The managing director may pause to speak to a worker on his tour round the assembly line. These are the relations we *see*, and since it is easier to understand things we see than things we do not, the mind naturally fixes on encounters of this kind when trying to identify class relations.

Class relations, however, are not directly discernible in the way that personal relations are. They are relations of groups rather than individuals, and in capitalist society they are mediated by money. At the risk of oversimplifying class relations in capitalist society, we can say that its typical relation is that of wage labour, in which those who own the means of production hire those who do not. Those whose only assets are personal ones — their physical and mental abilities — can make a living only by working for a wage. Those whose assets include buildings and machinery (in a word, capital) can make a living by setting people to work on them. You cannot *see* this relation directly by watching people at work, or even by seeing the director in conversation with the worker on the assembly line. To this extent class relations are abstract, and some degree of reflection is necessary if one wants to discern them.

Marx expressed this in a paradoxical way: 'Society does not consist of individuals; it expresses the sum of connections and relationships in which individuals find themselves.'[2] By this he meant that society is the pattern of class relations rather than the face-to-face contacts between individuals, and that this pattern is abstract rather than concrete. Individuals 'find themselves' in these relationships because they are born into a particular class, and the class they are born into determines to a greater or lesser extent their place in society.

In practice one's position in society has a considerable influence on one's personal life — something I shall say more about later. In theory, however, it is possible to distinguish between social relations and personal relations, even to the extent of saying that much of one's personal life takes place *outside of* the social relations in which one find oneself. In a sense we are persons outside social relations — inside them we are members of a particular class.

Politics

'Politics' comes from *polis*, the Greek word for a city-state, and when Aristotle said that man is a political animal he meant that man is a creature of the *polis*. In the Athenian *polis*, at the high point of its development, all free adult male citizens had the right to take part in its business, and although this participation was limited (since it excluded women, slaves and aliens), it was a special kind of democracy. The assembly, which dealt with legislation and justice, was controlled by all male citizens who wanted to attend. There were no specialists or professionals in any of these spheres — no judges or civil servants — and the council, which prepared the assembly's agenda, was chosen by lot. Thus every citizen had the opportunity to take part in *polis* life. It was a direct rather than a representative type of democracy, and is similar in certain respects to the type of participatory democracy that modern socialists have pursued. *Polis* life meant more than just the assembly: it had connotations of 'the community' and 'the people', and being a political animal meant participating fully in the life of the city. It was not only a duty that the citizen owed the city, it was a duty he owed himself, for the Greeks believed that the individual who leads only a private existence is not fully human. *Polis* life was not only political life as we understand it; it was also public life. It included not only the assembly, but also religious ritual, the theatre and public debate.

Politics later came to have the more specialised meaning of the science and art of government. It has, by extension, come to mean the regulation of bodies other than the state, such as businesses. We now talk of board-room politics or the internal politics of a party — notions which would have been meaningless to the Greeks. Politics in this sense requires one to organise in order to exert influence, and is inseparable from the formation of caucuses and groupings. Whether an organisation is hierarchical or egalitarian, tyrannical or libertarian, anyone who wants to influence what happens in it has to be political — 'to find allies, to speak persuasively, to gain votes and to disarm opponents.

The type of politics varies with the type of organisation. Brutal organisations, for example, have brutal internal politics. In the National Front internal conflicts have included the stabbing of an unpopular leader. Quakers, by contrast, not only oppose force but also voting. Decisions are taken by the feeling of the meeting, and eloquence, seniority and reputation count for more than the ability to organise ballots.

A lot of people dislike politics because of the organising it involves. Even people who consider themselves politically-minded sometimes dislike politics and aspire to a society where politics in this sense no longer exists. They feel it is too Machiavellian, dishonest and formal. But the absence of formal structure does not do away with politics; it only makes it more surreptitious. The characteristic political process of unstructured organisations is a subtle pressure to conform. Jo Freeman, in a perceptive commentary on politics in the women's movement, has called this pressure the tyranny of structurelessness.[3] Formal structures are necessary to guard against this pressure.

Politics is not just about the state and parliament, laws and ministries, parties and elections. It is about the exercise of influence and power and the way one exercises them. Politics exists in all groups and organisations, and one of the achievements of the personal politics movement has been to show that you can find it in the private sphere as well as the public — in the family, in sexual relations and in personal relations. Areas of life that were once thought to be non-political are now recognised as political. Where 'political' used to mean only 'connected with a political party', it now means 'involving the exercise of power and influence'.

Power and society

Politics and social relations are not the same thing. If we do not distinguish one from the other, we will fall into confusion:

> Because we have lived so intimately with our oppressors, in isolation from each other, we have been kept from seeing our personal suffering as a political condition. This creates the illusion that a woman's relationship with her man is a matter of interplay between two unique personalities, and can be worked out individually. In reality, every such relationship is a *class* relationship, and the conflicts between individual men and woman are political conflicts that can only be solved collectively.[4]

This passage makes the important point that it is usual for people to regard the relations between men and women as *purely* personal, and usual for them to overlook the fact that they are social as well — that is, a relation between two groups forming part of the social structure. It also makes the point that there are relationships of power between men and women, but it does not distinguish this point from the first one, and so implies that gender relations are social *because* they are political. The assumption behind this is that if relations between individuals are political they must be social, and therefore they cannot be personal.

Other writers state explicitly that all relations of power are social relations. For example, one author defines politics as 'relationships between people and between groups of people from the micro level, i.e. interpersonal relationships, up to the macro government and state adminstration level.'[5] Here politics is confused with relationships as such. But politics is not relationships as such. It is the power, and methods of organising power, that *runs through* relationships of different kinds. The connection between politics and relationships is rather like the connection between an electric current and a cable: the current runs through the cable and politics runs through the relationships, but the cable is not an electric current and relationships are not politics.

Politics does not exist only in government and public life, it also exists in personal relations and private life. There are really two kinds of politics — the kind that pertains to social relations and the kind that pertains to personal relations: social politics and personal politics. Just as social life and personal life are connected, so personal politics and social politics are connected as well; but just as social relations are distinct from personal relations, so social politics are distinct from personal politics. Personal politics fades imperceptibly into psychology; social politics does not.

The extreme versions of personal politics overlook the fact that there are two kinds of politics. You can say 'the personal is political' and use it as an excuse for putting all your energies into personal relations, but you thereby turn your back on social politics.

One of the things that makes it hard to see the distinction between the personal and the social is the problematic nature of the relations between the sexes. Are they personal or social? They involve face-to-face relations, so to that extent they are personal, but they are also relations between two groups, so to that extent they are social. They occupy an ambiguous position, neither exclusively personal nor exclusively political.

Gender relations

It is not hard to see how the illusion grew up that a woman's relationship with her man is no more than a matter of interplay between unique personalities, for that is the impression created by erotic relations between the sexes.*

In every romantic film or novel love first blossoms when a couple escape from the crowd and find themselves alone for the first time. Heroes steer heroines to moonlit balconies where each declares undying love for the other. We all know this romantic world to be false, but there does seem to be some truth in the idea that solitude is necessary for love and sex. However, even in erotic relations there is something more than the relations of two individuals. Freud, who more than anyone else has torn the romantic veil from heterosexual love, said that in any relationship between a man and a woman, six people are involved — the man and the woman themselves, and their four parents. That is an interpretation of the psychological reality. The social reality is more complex. Into a relationship between two individuals enter ghosts and stereotypes born of the experiences of generations. Behind each man stands the male sex, behind each woman the female sex. An erotic relation is not just the relation of two individuals: it is the relation of two sexes.

This becomes plain for women who suffer at the hands of men. We have little reason to look below the surface of our lives when everything is going well, but when things go badly we begin to wonder and to analyse. Because things have gone so badly for so many women they have looked beneath the surface and seen the contours of a social relation. Erotic relations are seen to be connected with other types of gender relations. Apparently unconnected things are revealed to be linked — inconsiderate love-making and the fact that men occupy most public offices, or low rates of pay for women and the fact that men interrupt women when they are speaking. The indignities and inequalities all form part of a social system, and the system, rather than individuals who find themselves in it, gives rise to women's disadvantages and men's advantages. Men are powerful not because they are innately superior, but because the system gives them power, and women are weak not because they are innately inferior, but because relations between men and

---

* I use the phrase 'erotic relations' because 'sexual relations' is too ambiguous. It means so many different things: the social relations between men and women, affection between individuals of different sexes and physical relations between individuals of the same sex. What I am concerned with are the relations between men and women, which I call 'gender relations' — rather a technical term, but one which clarity demands. The physical and emotional relations between men and women — 'erotic relations' — are one instance of gender relations.

women makes them so.

One cannot perceive the system in which men and women are caught unless one considers the male and female population — considering individuals alone will reveal little. When one considers women's place in the labour market, for instance, one can see that they form a subordinate group in relation to men similar to the subordinate group workers form in relation to employers. In Britain in 1979 more than half the married women under 45 worked, and three-fifths of those between 45 and sixty did, and the proportions have been rising steadily since 1951. By and large, women go to work for financial reasons, but they tend to earn less than men.[6] The average weekly earnings of British male manual workers in 1979 were about £97, those of female manual workers about £58 — 60 per cent of what men earned.[7]. The status of women workers is lower than that of men, the most telling illustration of which is the fact that the overwhelming majority of secretaries are women, but only a tiny number of managers. (Ten years ago in the USA the figures were 97 per cent and 2 per cent respectively.[8]) And just as women do badly when they are in work, so they are particularly badly affected when unemployment goes up, tending to be among the first affected by redundancies.

The problems women face outside waged work also reveal their subordinate position. Nearly all women who do waged work are also responsible for domestic work and child-care as well, and when the amount of time they spend on this is added to the amount of time they spend working for a wage, we see the number of hours they spend working every week to be very high indeed. Seventy hours is not unusual. If women want to do paid work outside the home, it is hard for them to find day care for their children, and in Britain only 2 per cent of working mothers with children under five have day nursery places. Even in families where the mother works full-time outside the home, fathers rarely take time off if the children are ill, and rarely collect them from school.[9]

It may be thought that this unwaged work of childcare and home-making is a personal, not a social thing, since it takes place in private. But it is social because, in its way, it contributes to the social relations of production as much as paid work does. A nice home, a filling meal, a clean change of clothes, and the wage-earner is restored. He returns to the daily grind better fitted to keep the wheels of industry turning and the piles of paper shuffled. Women's disadvantages as workers and as wives are of a piece, and so it is hard not to conclude that they are part of a system, and that the relations between the sexes are social.

Socialists and feminists agree that women's disadvantages arise from social relations, but they disagree about whether these relations are economic or sexual. Are women's disadvantages purely the result of the economic system — either of private property in general or capitalism in particular — or are they the result of patriarchy, the social relations of women and men?

Patriarchy

Marxists usually feel uncomfortable with the notion of patriarchy. One of the fundamental ideas of Marxism is that in the last resort all social relations originate from the means of production. The idea that there might be social relations that are *not* based on the means of production is a fundamental challenge to Marxism, and the notion of patriarchy asserts just that.

The traditional Marxist view is that feminism is mistaken and diversionary, and that was the view Lenin took of the feminism of his time. Lenin spoke bitterly about German women who took it upon themselves to fight the sexual oppression that male socialists ignored. They held meetings in which they discussed problems that affected them deeply — problems of marriage, sexuality and personal relations. Lenin's response showed a failure to recognise the importance of social relations other than economic ones. He thought the meetings were at best irrelevant, at worst counter-revolutionary. He thought the women's interest in sexual life was bourgeois, and their desire for sexual freedom debilitating. 'The revolution demands concentration, increase in forces, from the masses, from individuals,' he thundered. 'It cannot tolerate orgiastic conditions such as are normal for the decadent heroes of D'Annunzio. Dissoluteness in sexual life is bourgeois, is a phenomenon of decay.' In a revealing phrase he spoke of people 'poking about in sexual matters', and he dismissed Alexandra Kollontai's glass-of-water doctrine, in which she expressed her belief that people should satisfy sexual desire in the same matter-of-fact way that they satisfy thirst. 'Of course thirst must be satisfied,' he objected, 'but will the normal man in normal circumstances lie down in the gutter and drink out of a puddle, or out of a glass with a rim greasy with many lips?'[10] Did Lenin speak of men drinking out of dirty glasses because he thought that they were contaminated by sexual contact with women? We cannot be sure, but there is surely something significant in the analogy he chose.

Some Marxists try and accommodate themselves to feminism in more or less far-fetched ways, one of the most common of which is the notion of women as a 'section of the working class'. 'Some sections of the working class suffer from a double oppression,' they say; 'for example, women are oppressed both *as members of the working class*, under capitalism, and *as women*.'[11] But this view is not easy to sustain.

What does it mean to say women are a 'section of the working class'? Surely it means that every woman is working class. It is not easy to justify such an idea. Is a duchess working class because the estate she lives off belongs to her husband? Is the wife of the chairman of the board working class because she has the responsibility of looking after the children? Either we can insist that such women *are* members of the working class, because they are oppressed as women, or we can say they are *not* oppressed as women because they are not members of the working class. Each alternative is unacceptable. The first makes nonsense of the idea of the working class by including in it the female part of the ruling class. The second makes nonsense of the idea of women as an oppressed group by excluding from it the upper-class part of the female sex.

The device of 'sections of the working class' will not do. It causes too much cramp. All women are oppressed as women, irrespective of their class. Working-class women are oppressed, both as workers and as women, but women who are not working-class are still oppressed as women. It is perfectly simple: there are two forms of oppression. This is precisely what many Marxists find difficult to accept. They are reluctant to acknowledge that women who are not working class might be oppressed.

There is another way some Marxists try to avoid accepting the reality of patriarchy, and that is by saying that although women are oppressed as women, this oppression is comparatively recent in origin, since it comes from capitalist production. But there is no shortage of evidence that women's oppression predates capitalism. We can look back in time to primitive society, and can see that at every stage men were on top.

The fact that women's oppression has taken a particular form under capitalism is what has led people to suppose that capitalism brought it about and that without capitalism it will vanish. But that patriarchy has been shaped in a particular way by capitalism does not mean it is, like the Stock Exchange, a capitalist institution, or that it draws sustenance only from the capitalist mode of production. The association between capitalism and patriarchy is more like that between the tides and a pebble worn smooth by them: although the pebble has taken a particular shape from the action of the tides, its substance is not dependent on its even having been in the sea. The tides could stop, the sea could run dry, and the pebble would remain. Similarly, although patriarchy exists in its present form only by virtue of capitalist influence, capitalism could vanish and patriarchy would persist. The relations between men and women are different from economic ones.

Sexual politics

Power runs through the social relations between men and women just as it runs through the social relations between classes. In that sense the politics of gender relations is a form of social politics: two sexes confront one another, and one has power over the other. Since there are social relations of power between the sexes, women's disadvantages cannot be removed without social changes, and that requires political activity of a fairly conventional type: meetings, conferences, campaigns, legislation, and so on. But as well as being social, sexual politics are personal. In some respects they are similar to class politics, in others they are quite different.

The relations between a boss and his workers are social and not personal. The members of one class do not need to have any personal contact with members of another class for class relations to exist. As capitalist firms have got bigger, boss and worker have come to have less and less contact. In the old days, the days of 'master and men', they came into quite close contact. In the world of multinationals, directors, far from personally directing the labours of their employees, have often not even been to the towns where they work.

Gender relations are different. There can be none without personal contact, and because they are borne on the personal relations of individuals it is even harder to see them as social. But once we have seen they are social, we should not forget they are personal as well.

Since gender relations are partly personal it is possible for men and women, in their personal relations, to escape their social conditioning. It is essential that they do so if there is to be any improvement in sexual relations. Gender relations cannot change in the same way that economic relations change: men cannot be 'overthrown' in the way that capitalists were overthrown in the Russian revolution. Nor are large numbers of women likely to secede from all relations with men, as separatists advocate. So some alteration in personal relations is needed. We need to form civilised personal relations, neither forgetting that they are set against a social background, nor pretending that nothing can be done about them. If that were the case the future of sexual relations would be a bleak, unending war of attrition.

3. Personal Life

If you arranged to meet a friend at Waterloo Station you would have good cause to be annoyed if she didn't turn up. But imagine your annoyance if someone else, completely unknown to you, turned up instead and said, 'I am your friend for the evening. Don't grumble about it. Everyone is much the same really, and I'm perfectly capable of performing the functions of friendship as well as anyone else. The person you expected has gone to Paddington instead, since acts of friendship can be performed anywhere on the earth's surface, and don't have to be done in any particular place.' You would insist that you do not want to meet just anyone: you want your friend, and you want her to be here. Sophisticated arguments about everyone being much the same are all very well, but they negate everything we take for granted about friendship and deny all that is personal about personal relations.

There has been a lot of talk about the personal in the personal politics movement, but little consideration of what it actually is. Remember the man who thought he was explaining his personal decisions when, in fact, he was analysing capitalism and patriarchy: he understood little of the nature of personal life, even though he was all for personal politics. The reason why personal politics has so often submerged personal life under social politics is that we do not have a sufficiently clear conception of the personal.

The whole thing about personal life is its particularity and its immediacy. It is a matter of *this* person in *this* place at *this* moment. That is why the rent-a-friend has little to do with personal relations. Because personal life is particular and immediate, it is hard to generalise about it. Generalisations fail to strike home. They slide off the personal like water off a duck's back. It is as if theories and personal life exist in different dimensions. It is not so much that theories about personal life are untrue as that they are irrelevant. The theories always trail behind, trying to grasp hold of the experiences that have already passed on and gone a step ahead.

Personal life is concrete and individual. Social life is not. It is abstract and it does not depend on particular individuals at all. Social theory is possible only because it makes generalisations about groups in which the particular individuals don't count for much. Generalisations are about groups, classes, sexes, populations, masses — they describe averages, trends and typical actions. Individual exceptions get ruled out in the average. They become, in the language of statistics, 'standard deviations'. In personal relations, however, the peculiarities count for everything and the averages for nothing. The deviations are never standard. For sociology, and for Marxist or feminist theory, the thing is to discover the typical family, the typical relations of reproduction, the typical mechanisms of patriarchy. For personal life the thing is to have the opportunity and possibility of living the way you want to live. When it comes to personal relations, theory is often inappropriate. The particular gets lost in the general, the individual in the typical. Listening to theories about personal life is often like looking at a table of statistics and trying to recognise oneself in a percentage.

Personal biographies

Each life follows its own course. Personal lives are unique, and for that reason the most appropriate way of talking about a life is biography or the novel. It is no accident that the feminist publishing houses have filled their lists with novels rather than textbooks, and it is no accident that most feminists feel more at home with a book by Marge Piercy than one by Karl Marx. They feel that they want as little as possible to do with the abstract theorising of the left. They feel that the texture of personal life gets lost in all that.

What makes a person individual is partly the peculiarities of character and physique, but it is very much more the uniqueness of her biography. Although we are all similar in many respects (and it is these similarities that count in sociology and psychology) our histories are different. Identical twins look alike, but even they have unique biographies.

Relationships as well as individuals have biographies. Relationships are similar in many respects, and perhaps there are only half a dozen different types — friendship, sexual love, the relationship between a parent and a child, the chance meeting of strangers, and so on; but the permutations of individuals make for an infinite variety of relationships. From the point of view of theory it is only the types of relationship that count, but from the point of view of life it is the different feeling of different relationships that count.

Sociologists have tried to write books about friendship, but what grandiose revelations of the obvious they are! Every friendship starts with a meeting, then there is a period of greater or lesser duration when the prospective friends get to know each other, then a degree of intimacy develops, and so on. When novelists trace the threads of particular friendships they, by contrast, can reach the heights. I am thinking for instance of the friendship of Aziz and Fielding in Forster's *A Passage to India*. Forster portrays the unfolding relationship between the Indian Moslem and the English agnostic. The way its thread is woven against the background of their respective cultures, against the ruination of Aziz by the English and Fielding's increasing alienation from his own people, the way the two men are shown to veer towards one another, and away, and together, makes it one of the finest portrayals of friendship there is. And I am thinking also of Virginia Woolf's *The Waves*, a sixfold biography, written from a subjective point of view, where the relations between Bernard and Susan and Rhoda and Neville and Jinny and Louis are refracted through the thoughts of each, starting with birth and going on through each one's life to their deaths. Both novels are thoroughly particular and thoroughly untheoretical.

Feminist consciousness-raising groups have made individual women realise they are not alone in their experiences, and this has been one reason for their success. Women find that the things they go through others go through too, and that things they are afraid to mention are spoken of by others. Consciousness-raising shows what is common to all and what is a part of our collective experience. But they also show the differences between people and the uniqueness of each biography, and there is a value in that as well. Being accepted for what one is, is no less important than sharing with others what all have in common.

Lovers, friends and enemies

Because personal relations are concrete there is little point in trying to make a theory of personal politics. Although I said at the outset that there are theoretical difficulties in the idea that the personal is political, and that I want to clarify the relation between them, I am not trying to write a theoretical book. In fact, one of the problems in the personal politics movement is that people theorise too much and fly off too readily into generalisations. My main point about personal relations is that one should not theorise about them, but should appreciate them. Otherwise the life is crushed out of them by the dead weight of abstraction.

So what can we say about personal relations? They involve particular individuals — we have seen that. They take place in particular places and at particular times — we have seen that too. They also persist over time, and as time passes the individuals in them may get to know more about each other. In relations of friendship and love the gradual getting to know each other is part of the pleasure of the relationship. If each person talks more about herself and gets to know more about the other, and if the details, the biography, the character rounds out, each person's sense of the other becomes firmer. Friends often want to spend time together without distraction, talking, doing things together, or not doing anything in particular. Silence is often as important as talking, and in relations that have matured people can enjoy one another's company without saying much at all.

Having got to know one another, friends develop trust and honesty. Relationships without trust and honesty are not real friendships. One has to feel that one can be honest about one's feelings, one's fears, one's weaknesses and one's fantasies without being ridiculed. The great virtue of old friendships, especially those which began in childhood or adolescence, is that one has neither the wish nor the ability to deceive one's friend. We already know all about each other, we know each other's character, and we know something of the events and experiences that have helped make us what we are.

We all need intimacy, to be close to people and to reveal our innermost thoughts and feelings honestly and without reserve. We need to love people and to be loved by them. It is a part of being human, and yet many people lack the ability to be intimate. The desire for power over others, or the fear of being betrayed, both prevent people being intimate. Or people confuse intimacy with sex, and think that if they are having a physical relation then they are being intimate. It is, however, quite possible to have a physical relationship without honesty, self-disclosure or even affection.

The personal politics movement has made a great deal of intimate relations. This is partly due to the lack of intimacy in the political organisations that feminists rebelled against. Traditional left organisations, especially revolutionary ones, have valued strength and toughness at the expense of openness and warmth of feeling. Cadre-type organisations have told their members to put political work first and personal relations second, treating intimacy as something bourgeois and sentimental. Intimacy has also been made much of in the personal politics movement because it has been excluded from many non-physical relations. Feminists have encouraged women to be more intimate with one another, and men who are interested in personal politics have encouraged men to be more intimate with one another as well. This is needed particularly in north America and northern Europe, where people tend to be very stiff and reserved anyway.

There is intimacy of varying kinds. The intimacy of lovers is bound to be different from the intimacy of friends. The intimacy between people who have known one another for a long time is bound to be different from the intimacy of people who have just become close — the former may not feel the need to be as demonstrative as the latter. Although the inability to form intimate relations is sad, people vary in their capacity and desire for intimacy. Some people like to be close to everyone they meet regularly, and form intimate relations very quickly, others like to be intimate with only a few people — perhaps only one person. Some people cease to be intimate as quickly as they have begun, moving from friend to friend in rapid succession. Others hang on tenaciously, dropping friends with reluctance, and then only for the most serious reasons. I don't think these variations in intimacy matter very much, and I see no reason why we should not accept wide differences in human relationships. We cannot set up standards determining the 'right' way to be intimate.

It is possible to sentimentalise personal relations by talking only about those which are based on affection. There are personal relations based on hatred too. Learning to hate an enemy gives some people as much pleasure as learning to love a friend. They gleefully discover her bad traits, weaknesses and failings. Hostility grows over time just as a friendship does, not bearing fruit, but ageing like an old cheese into something rancid and leathery. People can take perverse pleasure in nurturing enmity, and find perverse satisfaction in having a good moan behind someone's back. Love and hatred are not always separate, and we can feel both emotions for the same person. There is no close relationship without conflict, and the inability to handle it is responsible for many bust-ups and disappointments. When psychologists and marriage-guidance counsellors report the importance of conflict in a relationship they often hit the headlines. 'Couples who fight together are couples who stay together — provided they know how to fight properly,' say the experts,[1] and however much these findings may be trivialised there is a considerable amount of practical value in them.

There are personal relations based on neither love nor hatred — in fact, on no particular feeling at all. That is easily overlooked when we concentrate on personal relations of the more intense kind. Not all relationships are intense; not only are there lovers and enemies, but also neighbours, work mates and acquaintances. People who deal with one another in an instrumental or a circumscribed way also have personal relations. What distinguishes personal from social relations is not intimacy, but face-to-face contact. Non-intimate relations are an important part of our lives, and if we are to see personal life whole we have to include them. In themselves they may not be significant, but our ability and opportunity for them contributes greatly to the quality of our lives.

There is much to savour even in the casual meeting, in the company of people we like but are not close to, or whose presence we enjoy but could not endure every hour of the day. Such relations can be spoiled by too much togetherness, and the desire to make them all passionate is like the desire to eat nothing but syrup. There are friendships of a special and limited kind, people whom we like doing a particular thing with, but not everything.

Subjective experience

Personal relations, whether they are close or casual, differ from social ones not only in that they involve face-to-face contact, but also in that they involve subjective experience. In social life an objective structure emerges out of individual acts. Social structure is not the relations of individuals one to another and is not immediately apparent in the experience of individuals. It has to be grasped by an effort of understanding. Personal relations on the other hand are nothing but the relations of individuals and, if they do not enter into consciousness and subjectivity they are not personal relations at all, merely physical proximity, like the knocking of billiard balls against one another. The subjective character of personal relations explains why they are impervious to theory. Theory treats of what is objective and cannot be reduced to individual experiences. One needs theory to grasp the social structure, but personal experience eludes the grasp of theory precisely because it is subjective.

Personal biography is in part the history of a person's subjective experiences, not just a list of events that happened. In a personal biography the life process itself — a person's growth, maturity, sexuality, ageing, sickness and death — is reflected in those experiences, and when we speak of the personal this reflection is often what we mean.

In the life process we see, as we did in friendship, things that are common to all. We see what is universally human — and more than human, for the life process is also our animal life. There are solitary individuals with no friends at all, but there is no-one who is not born, who does not grow and who does not die. Because one's experience of the life process is an experience of what is universal, it is tempting to say the personalness of these experiences is illusory, a trick of self-centredness that stops us seeing what we share together. But seeing that certain events are common to us all does not mean being blind to the experiences that make a person's life unique.

Orthodox medicine seems to be coming under increasing criticism from medical practitioners who say it is the person, not the symptom, that doctors should treat. Most fringe medicines are united in the belief that the whole person should be healed. Homeopaths match the drug to the case. Osteopaths, naturopaths and acupuncturists all try and make the whole person strong enough to fight disease by means of her body's defences. Good medical practice, of whatever variety, has to have a sound grasp of general principles, understanding what is universal, but it also has to meet the individual case. The patient must be seen as a person, rather than the manifestation of a universal condition. The experiences of a person's life have to be seen like this as well: not just a manifestation of what is common to all, but what is peculiar to that individual.

The troubles we face in our personal lives have to be recognised as personal troubles. To many people that will seem obvious. How could anyone deny it? It should be obvious, but to some people it is not, and they do deny it. In political circles we often hear people condemning 'personal solutions'. The very phrase has become abusive. You should not seek personal solutions, they say; you should seek social ones.

When people condemn personal solutions they generally do so for two reasons. The first is that it is not practicable to seek personal solutions, because only social change will get rid of personal troubles. The troubles we suffer in our personal lives, they say, are caused by the type of society we live in and the sort of social relations that prevail in it, and if you go for a personal solution all you do is integrate yourself into an unsatisfactory society without touching the cause of your problems. The second reason is that it is morally wrong to go for personal solutions, because to do so is to ignore the problems other people suffer and to find some personal satisfaction at others' expense.

As to the first reason, it all depends on the particular case. If your personal trouble is a fear of nuclear war, you do not solve it by ridding your mind of it and pretending to yourself that there is no real danger. But in other cases a personal solution may be perfectly feasible. If your personal problem is that you are socially isolated, finding it difficult to make friends, it may well be that the causes lie in yourself. Perhaps you have a low opinion of yourself, do not recognise the good qualities you have, do not take any initiative, and expect other people to make the first move in any relationship. In this case, to say your problems are all caused by society, and that if only people were not so alienated it would be possible for you to make friends, is simply bad faith. There are many personal troubles whose solutions lie in the individual, and although she may not find them without the help of others, they really *are* personal.

The second reason is really an appeal to altruism. It says you should not seek personal solutions because to do so is selfish and shows indifference to the problems of others. The way this is often put is to say it is 'individualistic'. I agree that, in general, people should be altruistic, but there is a difference between being altruistic and neglecting your personal needs. I think the trouble is that some people who are committed socialists — and even some people who are committed feminists — do not appreciate the importance of self-love. If you do not love yourself and do not treat yourself kindly, not only are you no good to yourself, you are no good to other people. Those who make harsh demands on themselves usually make harsh demands on others as well. Indeed, there is a case to be made *against* altruism, for altruism can take the form of a commitment to high social ideals that overlooks individuals and their needs and weaknesses.

Some feminists condemned Agnes Varda's film *One Sings, The Other Doesn't* because its two heroines found their solutions in personal life rather than sisterhood. Both women had problems that many women face, and were shown living their lives and seeking happiness rather than submerging themselves in collective action. In the eyes of its critics the film made the wrong point: it showed it was possible to find happiness in one's personal life.

The demand to eschew personal solutions resurrects self-sacrificing politics. It shows a failure to recognise what personal relations are and what personal politics means. Personal politics does not just mean showing the social background of personal life; it also means making individuals the real ends of political action.

Eschewing personal solutions can go to ridiculous lengths. I know of a couple who decided they would sleep together only after the revolution. They decided that the evils of capitalism and patriarchy enter so deep into the soul that there is no prospect of decent human relationships in this society. It is hardly believable that anyone should be so fanatical, but this couple do illustrate the logical conclusion that the refusal of personal solutions leads to. There is always bad faith in this kind of fanaticism, always confusion and self-deception. The arguments about patriarchy and capitalism must always strike you as somehow beside the point, for there is a disproportion between the supposed facts about society that people like this adduce and the extremity of their conclusions. I believe that people who are capable of turning their backs on personal life so completely would have unhappy personal lives *in any society*, and that the more they rail against personal solutions, the more they show their problems to be personal rather than social. For by saying that the precondition of solving the problems in your personal relations is the total overthrow of capitalist and patriarchal relations you provide yourself with a cast-iron excuse for doing nothing about your personal life.

Finding personal solutions is not, however, 'non-political'. But just as personal relations are different from social relations, so the politics of personal relations are different from social politics. If we can understand the difference between the two types of politics we may be able to avoid the errors of revolutionary puritanism and understand how necessary personal solutions are.

4. The Politics of Personal Relations

'The capitalist mode of production [has] to be revolutionised before meaningful relationships [can] be established.'[1] This view is not uncommon on the far left and exemplifies the hostility to personal solutions we often find there. It is intended as a statement of fact, but it is really a moral statement. 'Because socialists have not recognised the personal crisis as an area for political work,' the author continues, 'a mixed bag of pundits have stepped in with their mystifying "solutions" — Masters and Johnson, R.D. Laing, etc.'[2] What he is concerned about, I am sure, is not that people are trying to establish meaningful relationships in circumstances where it is impossible but that they are succeeding at the expense of political action. What he is concerned about is that people have benefitted from the psychological pundits in areas where socialists have had little to offer them. Urging socialists to politicise personal life can only mean encouraging a social intervention in personal solutions.

The mechanical prescriptions of sexologists like Masters and Johnson may have mystified personal relations, but it is hard to see how Laing ever did. In his psychiatric work and his writings he has tried to remove the mystifications that surround behaviour and experience, and to restore to people a clearer sense of themselves and their desires. The idea of making the personal crisis an area of political work is far more mystifying than any psychological theory, for by 'political work' this writer, and many who think like him, means social politics. He effectively denies that personal relations are different from social relations or that personal politics are different from social politics. It is far more mystifying to suggest that the processes of personal politics are the same as those of social politics than to try and discover what the processes of personal politics are.

In personal relations individuals exert power over each other. The means they use range from subtle glances, double messages, interruptions of speech, dominating gestures and control of personal space to violence, rape and murder.

The irrational in politics

We control others both by what we say and the way we say it. The issuing of orders is too obvious to need elaboration, but we control others by simple statements of fact as well. Control means not only getting others to *do* something, it also means getting others to *be* something we want them to be. It is possible to get people to be what we want them to be by telling them that they *are* as we wish them to be, and by a process comparable to hypnosis they eventually come to conform. This result can be achieved even by telling a third party in their presence what they supposedly are. Naturally, a certain kind of relationship is necessary for this to work, and it is often present in families. Laing has described this process in the following words:

> One way to get someone to *do* what one wants, is to give an order. To get someone to *be* what one wants him to be, or supposes he is or is afraid he is (whether or not this is what one wants), that is, to get him to embody one's projections, is another matter. In a hypnotic (or similar) context, one does not tell him what to *be*, but tells him what he is. Such *attributions*, in context, are many times more powerful than orders (or other forms of coercion or persuasion). An instruction may not be defined as an instruction... Your word is my command. A relationship of one to another may be of such power that you become what I take you to be, at my glance, at my touch, at my cough. I do not need to say anything.[3]

Thus a parent may say of her child, 'Marion is a self-conscious little girl. She gets embarrassed by people speaking about her — don't you Marion?' The girl gets embarrassed when she hears this. Eventually the parent is able to communicate her intentions by means of a glance, a touch, or a cough. Hypnotic gestures of this kind affect deeper layers of the psyche than the gestures that assert superiority.

There is a law that goes deeper than the laws of social politics. There is, says Laing, a law of feelings, desires, hopes, fears, perception, imagination and dreams. If these do not correspond to the law, they are outlawed and excommunicated. The law that operates in certain families, and the processes used to secure conformity to it, may so rob individuals of autonomy that they become incapable of living their lives. In *Sanity, Madness and the Family* Laing and Esterton have described such families and the way they control their members. An understanding of these processes can deepen our understanding of the politics of personal relations.

There is more to personal politics than control and domination, however. The personal politics movement is inclined to see personal relations in only one dimension. It runs the gamut of personal politics from A to B, seeing little but oppression on one side and liberation on the other. The subtleties, contradictions, ambiguities and self-deceptions are lost to view. In applying a single criterion to personal relations — the criterion of oppressiveness — the personal politics movement has tended to develop a restricted vision that does not help as much as it ought to. The knots that people tie themselves into, the games they play and their denial of each other's autonomy, are overlooked.

Personal politics involve our perceptions of our own and of others' behaviour, the way we act on those perceptions, and the way others act on their perceptions of us. In personal relations each person's understanding of the other contributes to the relationship. The way we interpret the behaviour of others is influenced by our past experience in our family and society. We bring to our relationships what we have learned outside them. That does not mean our relationships are completely determined by our past histories or by the social relations in which we are embroiled. History and society are not fate, and we are not condemned always to suffer our lives as they have been made for us. Understanding what occurs within them gives us the power to alter them.

Many unsatisfactory relationships get caught in a vicious spiral of 'mismatched interpretations, expectations, experiences, attributions and counter attributions'.[4] These spirals include so many levels of perception that the individuals in them are usually unaware of them. They include my perception of you, your perception of me, my perception of your perception of me, your perception of my perception of you, and so on. Sometimes they are comparatively easy for an outsider to unwind, sometimes they are more difficult. For example, a woman may feel safe with a man because he does nothing; she may be angry with him because he does nothing; he may not frighten her because, doing nothing, he is useless. *Because* she feels safe with him she may despise him; and she may cling to him *because* he does not frighten her. She may despise him because she clings to him because he does not frighten her.[5]

It may seem that these aspects of interpersonal perception have little to do with politics, but personal politics are not like social politics. Power in personal relations is not just a matter of oppression. The irrational has its place. As Laing puts it, 'I... tend to select others for whom I can be the other that I wish to be, so that I may then reappropriate the sort of meta-identity I want.'[6] In gender relations women often select men in whose eyes they appear as they wish to appear in their own eyes. That accords with what we know about the conditioning which makes women become the women *men* want them to be. But there are personal relations between men and women different from these. Thus, there are women who despise their men because they do nothing, who are angry with them because they do not frighten them, and so on. And there are men who want women to dominate and despise them. There are both men and women who court rejection, playing the game of Kick Me. Eric Berne has found that a man who plays Kick Me behaves in such a way that he seems to be saying to everyone around him, 'Please don't kick me.' The temptation becomes irresistible, and when the inevitable result follows, the player cries, 'But the sign says "*Don't* kick me".' Then he adds incredulously, 'Why does this always happen to me?'.[7]

Every relationship is made of layers of experience, perception and fantasy. Into every relationship there enters, to some degree or other, self-deception, misperception or double meaning. We are motivated by unconscious wishes and fantasies. We respond inappropriately to what is going on around us and send our relationships crashing into the wrong gear.

Space invaders

The *way* things are said often escapes our attention, but it influences us as much as *what* is said. We respond not only to undertones of speech, but also to gestures and other non-verbal signs. These non-verbal signs have been studied by psychologists, and there is a large body of literature on the subject, but psychologists have tended to overlook the fact that by means of these signs people control one another. Nancy Henley, a psychologist at Lowell University, has reviewed much of this literature and has revealed the political aspects of gesture, touch, demeanour, eye contact, facial expression, spatial relations and the undertones of speech.

Henley argues that the social structure of an authoritarian society is maintained by means of power in personal relations. Only by maintaining a particular type of personal relation can an authoritarian society persist. In other words, there is a relationship between social politics and personal politics. She descibes this relationship in the following way:

> In front of and defending the political-economic structure that determines our lives and defines the context of human relationships, there is the micro-political structure that helps maintain it. This micropolitical structure is the substance of our everyday experience. The humiliation of being subordinate is often felt most sharply and painfully when one is ignored or interrupted while speaking, towered over or forced to move by another's bodily presence, or cowed unknowingly into dropping the eyes, the head, the shoulders. Conversely, the power to manipulate others' lives... or plan the bombing of far-off peasants is conferred in part by others' snapping to attention in one's presence, their smiling, fearing to touch or approach, their following one around for information or favours. These are the trivia that make up the batter for that great stratified waffle that we call our society.[8]

Power is associated with space. The rich and powerful have larger houses and gardens than the poor and powerless. They also have more space at work, those at the bottom of the hierarchy working in small cramped offices, those at the top having very large ones. Not only do the rich and powerful have more space: the space they occupy is of better quality. Suburbs are not as polluted as slums. They have less industry, more trees and parks, and fewer trucks drive through them. In London, there has been a long association of high ground (such as Hampstead) with high status, and low ground (such as Southwark) with low status. In Guyaquil, the largest city in Ecuador, the rich live on dry land and the poor in mangrove swamps. This association of space with power exists in personal life as well. In the home, men commonly have more space than women, and are more likely to have their own study or workshop.

The space around a person's body is also associated with power. To move very close to another person is to exert power over her, to force someone to move out of this personal space is to resist the exercise of power. Certain people may be permitted to enter this personal space in certain circumstances: a lover may move within six inches of one's body without causing offence; if a stranger in the street does the same thing, the act creates a sense of violation. In relations of dominance and submission, the dominant person expands and invades the space of the other, while the submissive person contracts and permits her space to be invaded. Men expand, women contract. Men sprawl, sit with legs apart, put their feet on the table, and lean back in chairs. Women put their knees close together, fold their arms across their breasts, and keep their elbows close to their sides. Dominating individuals stand in high places or tower over those they dominate. Those who are dominated sit down or bow their heads. Insight into the significance of space and superiority inspires certain business deals. African peddlers on Mediterranean beaches will squat on their haunches when sunbathers show an interest in their wares. To remain standing during the course of negotiations would be to make the purchaser feel dominated. To make her feel that it is she who is dominating, the peddler crouches to denote inferiority. Thus the purchaser, even if she ends up paying more than she would pay in the shops, will feel she has won the exchange with the peddler.

Dominance is also communciated by gestures. Standing erect with hands on hips is a familiar way of letting others know you are in charge. A relaxed body is the sign of being in control, a tense one the sign of being controlled. (Imagine the relaxed superior reclining in a swivel chair behind his desk while the cowed subordinate stands rigid before him.) Women tighten their jaw muscles in the presence of men. The significance of gestures varies from culture to culture. Young American blacks show defiance of authority by loosening their limbs and becoming more and more relaxed as a conflict continues; young whites adopt a different stance, body rigid, legs spread apart, arms still and fists clenched.

Gestures which we think of as gestures of affection are gestures of control as well, as is made plain by the fact that men and women use different gestures of affection towards each other. A man will put his arm round a woman's shoulder, but a woman will take a man's arm. Superiors put their arms round the shoulders of subordinates, but the gesture may not be reciprocated. The foreman may put his arm round the worker as an act of friendly persuasion, but the worker may not put his arm round the foreman in an act of friendly defiance. Many forms of touch are ambiguous, connoting affection and superiority in varying measures, and social order is maintained by overlooking the current of power that flows through a touch. Interestingly enough, women — who are commonly thought to touch a great deal more than men — do so less. In public places, touch is usually initiated by those with higher status and more social power. In mixed-sex groups, two-thirds of all physical contact is initiated by men, and only a third by women. When old and young people are together, four-fifths of all contacts are made by the older person, a fifth by the younger. Those with high status touch those with low status three times as much as the other way round. Touching is also associated with dominant personalities: unassertive people touch less than assertive ones.[9]

In public places there are personal relations between strangers, and personal politics enter into them. I call these relations personal because they involve face-to-face contact, which is the essence of personal relations, even though in common usage we describe them as impersonal because they are lacking in intimacy. It may seem eccentric to describe the relations between strangers as personal, but the distinction I have been making between abstract social relations and concrete personal relations requires that we do so. We cannot describe them as social, because social relations are the relations between groups that make up the social structure, and this sort of encounter in a public place is not a relation between groups. What I am saying is that, in order to understand the personal and the political, we need to look at personal relations in a slightly different way from usual, as relations that cover a broad range of personal contacts from the most lasting and intimate to the most fleeting and casual, and we need to look at personal politics in a similar way. In the intimate and casual alike, similar political processes can be seen. The patronising gesture a man makes to a woman in a public place is comparable to the affectionate touch between a man and his wife. There is a social repertoire of male-female gestures, and even though the same gesture may *seem* to have a different meaning in different contexts, similar gestures express similar power relations. Increasing our awareness of personal politics involves becoming aware of these currents of power that are expressed in gestures, whether between intimates or strangers, whether in private or public.

Personal politics in social organisations

The arena of social politics is a public one, and the matters dealt with there are different from the political matters of private life. Yet the political matters of private life can be found there too, for in this public arena, where regional, national and even international matters may be decided upon, there are face-to-face contacts and therefore personal politics. Beneath the high-voltage social politics on the agenda there is the quiet hum of personal politics, sometimes unnoticed and frequently unacknowledged. We need to be aware of it here as much as anywhere else. We need to look at who speaks and who is silent, who is raised upon a stage and who sits below, who looks down and who looks up, who touches and who is touched, who stares and who looks away. And we need to be aware of the operation of irrationality and fantasy as well, the way people in a political organisation may seem to be pursuing the objects they speak about when they are really pursuing something else, some unconscious will-o'-the-wisp.

We need to get rid of the petty tyrannies and the fantasy objects. This is not easy. To talk of them in a political organisation is to meet incomprehension and resistance. And where do we find the space to introduce such matters as these? The incomprehension, the resistance, the lack of space — these are the reasons why so many women have left male-dominated socialist organisations. And there is a genuine problem here, because the *social*-political objects of an organisation *do* have to be pursued, and it would be quite wrong to sacrifice them to the personal. These problems are most acute for women, but they exist for men as well, for among men age may dominate youth, experience newness, self-confidence unassertiveness, just as masculinity

dominates femininity. And there is the sheer bewilderingness of
most political organisations to the newcomer.

When I first joined the Labour Party I certainly found it
bewildering. I was new to this kind of organisation, all my
previous political experience came from single-issue campaigns
and community politics. I had been used to informal meetings
where enthusiasm was all that was needed to get you involved. I
found the Labour Party, by contrast, formal and intimidating.
It has a complex structure and complex rules and a constitution
that everyone refers to but no-one explains, and which to this
day I don't fully understand. My only consolation is that most
other members are probably as vague about it as I am, moving
as if in a fog where visibility is restricted to the things that are
close up, and where things further away (what *is* the connection
between the regional councils and the NEC?) loom dimly and
then vanish. I attended a meeting of my constituency party's
general committee for the first time, and found a crowded agenda
taken at a cracking pace, and everyone discussing things I knew
nothing about. I found a male language of 'brothers' and 'chairman' and women officers signing themselves 'yours fraternally'.
I also, I should say, found as decent a bunch of people as you
will find anywhere, and a lot more decent than most.

I have also been in organisations where there is less decency,
and where people's wish to perceive themselves in a certain way,
or their passion for controlling others, actually disrupts the
organisation. I have, for several years, been active in a residents'
association which is fighting the council's wish to destroy a community without consulting the people in it. It is one of those
traditional organisations whose founders conceive of democracy
as the election of officers rather than the participation of
members. It is a small organisation, so the participation of
members would be quite practicable, but the committee permits
them to meet only once a year. Most of the members are elderly
people who dread the demolition of streets they have known for
thirty years or more. They are not politically sophisticated, they
trust their leaders and elect them year after year, and this trust
allows the leaders to be big fish in a small pond, and to compen-
sate for their lack of power in fighting the council by exercising
power over the members. The chairperson presides over the annual meeting with the unctious manner of a Sunday school
teacher, and does his best to keep discussion to a minumum. The

secretary dashes about from place to place with ever-growing bundles of paper and becomes more like a council officer every day. My attempts to open up the organisation, to make it more democratic and to involve all the members, have always been taken by the committee-men as a personal attack on them. The personal current in this small organisation pops and crackles with an unusually high voltage.

In neither of these organisations — the big national one and the small local one — is personal politics on the agenda, so the subtle controls in the personal relations of social politics get exercised almost unawares.

I say we need to change things, and that means it is not enough to withdraw from unpleasant organisations. Becoming a political abstainer, or confining oneself to personal politics, simply means giving up social politics. One way these things might be changed is by the formation of women's caucuses within political organisations. Such caucuses have recently been formed in the Labour Party. They fight against government policies that hit women hardest, against sexism in the labour movement, and for positive discrimination in the Labour Party. Women's caucuses are important because women suffer worst from the sort of personal oppression I have been talking about. There is no reason, however, why men's groups and mixed-sex groups should not also formed within the labour movement. They too can take up masculinity in social politics, ways to combat sexism, or methods of balancing the demands of the agenda and the needs of the individual.

Personal life and political principles

There is a space between two-person relations and the complicated relations of a mass organisation, a space in which the processes of personal politics show up particularly well. I mean the space occupied by small groups. In small groups there are politics of a slightly different kind from those that occur between couples. All the processes that occur in the relationship between two people can occur in a small group, but in the group there are political issues of a more familiar and less private kind. Nevertheless they remain personal as long as all the individuals in the group meet face-to-face. The politics of groups assume particular importance in collective living.

When people choose to live collectively for political reasons they choose to abandon traditional patterns of living and conventional solutions. They bring to the collective a refined political consciousness. Each difficulty that arises has to be dealt with afresh, and some harmony has to be established between political principles and personal relations. Any attempt to apply principles from social politics in a mechanical way, however, is bound to fail, since personal relations cannot be handled in the same way as organisations.

In a short account of the irritations and jealousies that plagued an American commune, Matthew Israel lists problems that will be familiar to anyone who has tried to live with other people. They illustrate the point I am making about principles. Betty kept the kitchen clean and tidy, but Sally always left it in a mess; this eventually reduced Betty to tears. Betty was keen on beautifying the house; Sally was indifferent to these artistic touches. Alice and Randy like simple surroundings, Jim accumulated large quantities of junk and irritated the others by his sloppy dressing and messy eating. The couples in the house ate late in the evening, sometimes not until ten; Matthew wanted to eat at six so he could go out with his friends. Communal meals took hours to prepare; Matthew wanted to eat quickly and get the meal over with. Matthew wanted to entertain alone; the meals were always eaten communally. Jim and Elaine were vegetarians and wanted a frugal diet; all the others were meat-eaters, and some wanted to spend a lot on food. Jim thought communal living meant everyone sharing everything; he lent Matthew's car to someone who did seven-hundred dollars' worth of damage to it. Betty like the thermostat at 68 degrees; Matthew liked it at 72; there were always arguments about it.[10]

I don't think anyone would claim to know how to solve all these conflicts. One thing ought to be fairly clear: there is no political principle that will determine whether thermostats should be set at 68 or 72 degrees. Principles governing personal life can be only of a general kind, they can never be applied to every conflict that arises. Unfortunately, authoritarianism sometimes comes in the guise of personal politics, such as when people imagine that you can use principles to govern every corner of personal life. They usually end up haranguing others for their low level of political consciousness or their bourgeois attitudes. My experience has been that collective households with the fewest principles have been the most harmonious. Whether there is a general lesson to be learned from that I am not sure, but I suspect there is.

Perfect harmony is a utopian dream, and some conflicts between individuals are bound to occur because of human diversity. That is not a pessimistic view of things, simply a recognition of the fact that the most important thing in personal relations is *getting on*, an unpredictable thing that is sometimes out of our control. When conflicts do occur the principles one can apply are those based on toleration and the need for self-assertiveness. But we ought not to deceive ourselves that personal politics is capable of solving every hitherto insoluble problem. The example of the thermostat shows the limits of strict principles. One can easily become the victim of one's one moral earnestness and over-simplify every snag so they all appear along the single dimension of oppression and liberation.

Personal politics means struggling against the personal oppressions we have assumed are normal, and questioning many things we take for granted. And it means suffering too, for it means change — wrenching ourselves from comfortable self-deceptions and cosy mistakes. But ultimately it means finding solutions: struggling and suffering, analysis of one's own motives and way of life are not ends in themselves.

We must not forget the danger of turning inward and of concentrating so much on the private, subjective and intimate that we forget the importance of public life. It may seem I have succumbed to this danger because I have been concentrating so much on personal solutions and personal psychology. I don't think I have. Although I have been talking about intimate relations I have not forgotten the non-intimate kind, and want to say something about them now. Intimate relations are important, but we have to understand that not all personal relations can or should be intimate. Too much intimacy weakens rather than enlivens public life.

5. The Cult of Intimacy

Personal politics has perceived the estrangement of modern public life, the silence and coldness of life in the city, and the flight into privacy. But it has misunderstood the problem, which it sees as the lack of intimacy in personal relations.

This is a mistake. To make all personal relations intimate would erode precisely those non-intimate relations upon which a vital public life depends. There was in the past a form of public life more vital and sociable than modern public life, a life which depended very much on a *lack* of intimacy. It was not the sort of public life we would want to emulate, because it was predominantly male and the product of class society. But there are some things we can learn from it, the most important of which is the value of a certain type of formality in public.

The inner-directed personality

The argument I am putting forward here goes against the accepted wisdom. It is commonly supposed that one of the problems of modern life is that formal and instrumental relations have increased at the expense of informal and expressive ones. David Riesman's book *The Lonely Crowd* described the emergence of an 'other-directed' personality for whom status and consumption are more important than genuine relationships. The loss of inner-directedness, said Riesman, has meant that although people mingle together they remain alone. Marriage-guidance counsellors George Bach and Peter Wyden express a similar view in *The Intimate Enemy*. People do not know how to be intimate with one another any more, they say. Married couples equate intimacy with sex, and do not realise that even though they have sex their marriage may still be devoid of intimacy. Intimacy, according to Bach and Wyden, is out of fashion.

> Movies, novels, and TV emphasise broken homes, broken dreams and cynicism — the failures of intimacy.

Organisation life, whether as a den mother or a corporation pyramid-climber, offers status, group identity and usually also money, and such rewards seem more attractive than the dimly perceived benefits of intimacy. No wonder people become emotional conservatives. They ask: why take an unnecessary risk? Intimacy looks to them like an investment in a high-risk stock; nice if you win, disastrous if you lose, and therefore best left alone.[1]

It is now a commonplace of liberal thinking that the world of 'the lonely crowd', 'the organisation man' and 'the status seekers' has robbed social life of intimacy. These phrases — each the title of a popular book from the fifties — have passed into the language and express an accepted view of modern society.

There was much of value in the critiques of Riesman, William H. Whyte (author of *The Organisation Man*) and Vance Packard (author of *The Status Seekers*), and if they called into question the ethos of corporate capitalism it was all to the good. They caught a mood that was to inspire the protest movements of the sixties. The disgust with the consumer society reached its zenith in the era of flower power and the rebellions of 1968. The liberal critiques of the fifties had a revolutionary counterpart ten years later in the writings of Marcuse and the Situationists. Personal politics also calls into question the mercenary relationships that spring out of corporate values.

The accepted wisdom has, however, led to a view of personal relations that makes us now value inner-directedness at the expense of outer-directedness. We think relationships appropriate to private life are equally appropriate to public life and casual meetings could be improved by warmer expressions of feeling. Richard Sennett, whose *Fall of Public Man* is a unique study of intimacy and public life, has shrewdly observed that the popularity of Riesman's book attests to an *increase* in the inner-directedness of American society, and a movement away from the very outer-directedness it describes.[2]

An entirely inner-directed personality is not conducive to sociability. A marriage that lacks intimacy is incomplete, and friends who are incapable of sharing themselves with one another run the risk of isolation. But the ability to enter into personal relations of a more casual kind — which may or may not develop into friendship — depends not on intimacy, but on sociability, which is a different thing. Since not all our relationships are close, we need rules of sociability. In other words, we need some degree of formality.

Informality

There has in the twentieth century been a tendency to greater informality in personal relations which has paralleled our preference for intimate relations. The dissolving of the stiffer sort of formality of the past was a good thing, because it really did inhibit the development of personal relations, but dissolving all formalities can impose on people a burden in the opening up of new personal relations.

There has been such a reaction against the older style of formality that we find much of that style grotesque. That husbands and wives could have addressed one another as 'Mr' and 'Mrs' in the privacy of their own homes strikes us now as absurd. The etiquette of visiting, which dominated the social life of the upper classes in the eighteenth and nineteenth centuries, seems like a charade today. Strict rules about who may visit whom, and at what stage in the relationship, and at what time of day seem to be not only unnecessary, but also positively damaging to real personal relations. We now feel that personal relations should be based on the very spontaneity that these rules were designed to prevent.

We take it for granted that formality means coldness and that sociability calls for spontaneity. It is true that there is a coldness and insensitivity in many public meetings and casual personal encounters. One of the revolutions effected by the women's movement has been in the way women relate to one another in public. It has melted the traditional hardness of political organisations and substituted warmth and friendliness. The impersonality of traditional political meetings is almost comical: the intensity of political argument is matched only by the weakness of personal contact. An ex-member of the Troops Out Movement, to take but one example, attributes its ineffectiveness to precisely this lack of personal contact:

> Occasionally 'socials' were organised to make money (she recalls). Grim they usually were too — Leftie men

> huddled in corners drinking pints and arguing about
> tactics and strategies, and each other. Often outsiders
> who came for a beer were either harangued or ignored.[3]

Anything would be an improvement on such unsociable socials.

What makes these meetings and get-togethers so unsociable is not their formality but their *informality*. There are few rules to facilitate the formation of personal relations. The informality that prevails in political organisations of this kind puts people together in public without any guidance concerning introduction or conversation. To engage with strangers in this sort of milieu demands eloquence or self-confidence, and those who lack it leave in silence and alone.

Formality has been discarded for a number of reasons. We have come to affect contempt for status, imagining that if the executive and the typist can address one another by their first names then they are somehow more equal. Another reason why we reject formality is that we consider relationships in which individuals do not reveal what they actually feel to be meaningless.

In the absence of formality, intimacy is the only possible foundation for a relationship. And once the formal conventions break down, the change affects everyone, for if those around you do not observe certain rules, you cannot continue to do so by yourself. The observation of social rules depends on public agreement that they should be observed. Rules of this kind are public and collective, not private and individual.

The absence of rules of formal intercourse does not mean there is an absence of any rules, for intimacy has rules of its own too. Certain forms of behaviour and ways of relating to other people become conventional, and in intimate gatherings there are rules of behaviour that can be as strict as the old formality. Hugging, for example, can become a ritual. In radical therapy circles it is often said that you hug only when you want to, but this particular expression of intimacy has, for some, become as much a formality as shaking hands.

The tyranny of structurelessness

One of the high points of intimacy in public is the party. Parties occupy an odd place in modern mythology. People love them and hate them at the same time. They swear they will never go to another party as long as they live — or for a couple of months.

The informal party, with its promise of excitement and romance, soon exerts its magnetism over the reluctant socialite. The sort of party I am thinking of is the one where it is too crowded to move, too loud to hear and too dark to see. All comers are set adrift to sink or swim in the social sea. There are no introductions and the evening has no structure. All have to make their own way and do their own thing. It's recreational Toryism. And yet, despite the fact that everyone is close together, there is nothing very sociable in a party. People are snogging in corners or huddling in boozy cabals, and if you want to enter into the life of the evening you have to hover on the fringe of a group you haven't been introduced to, waiting for the appropriate moment to drop the appropriate remark. Many people swim, but others sink, and at every such party I have been to there has been at least one person who spends the evening alone with a plastic cup.

Informality brings intimacy in its train because it demands that individuals enter into all relations sincerely, by means of self-disclosure and with their whole selves. Sincerity, self-disclosure and complete involvement are what mark out intimate personal relations from non-intimate ones. Sincerity means the whole truth about oneself without art or artifice. Self-disclosure means the revelation of feelings, emotions and reactions. The whole self means holding nothing back, an absence of reserve or covering up.

The cycle of attraction and repulsion many of us feel about parties comes from the demand for intimacy in circumstances where it is inappropriate, followed by a disappointment at how unsatisfying everything was.

Parties occupy an ambiguous position between the private and the public realm. Political organisations are, by contrast, clearly public. Despite the fact that there is often a formality about the conduct of meetings, there is rarely any formality in the engagement of the people who attend. Once again, newcomers have to sink or swim. The ritual familiarity of many public events certainly needs to be given more thought. Simply going round in a circle allowing each person to say who she is, or merely addressing one another as 'comrade' does not make these events more sociable. The introductions of the opening moments of a meeting are easily forgotten, and 'comrade' can be used as much to express hostility, in an ironical way, as it can to express sociability.

The sort of warmth and intimacy created in feminist circles has done a great deal to overcome the indifference to individuals in traditional politics, and a lot can be learned from it. But warmth alone, without some structuring of sociability, is not enough, and it has its own dangers. If intimacy becomes a cult it can be as inimical to real sociablity as the old ritual of visiting. We need to recognise the need for different types of personal relations based on different degrees of intimacy. If openness, sincerity, and complete involvement are valued *at the expense of* reserve, distance, partial engagement and artifice, and if these latter qualities are considered to be political vices or expressions of psychological inadequacy, public life suffers.

Jo Freeman pointed out in *The Tyranny of Structurelessness* that there is really no such thing as a completely structureless group, and that unstructured groups have a hidden and informal structure based on friendship elites. These elites are self-recruiting and self-perpetuating, and their members are selected because they possess preferred qualities that may have nothing to do with the political aims of the group. Such groups also have informal rules about how decisions are made. 'Those who do not know the rules,' says Freeman, 'and are not chosen for initiation must remain in confusion, or suffer from paranoid delusions that something is happening of which they are not quite aware.'[4] *The Tyranny of Structurelessness* is as relevant today as it was ten years ago because the preference for informality still persists, and although there have been many changes in the women's movement since it was written, the ideas that have spread from the movement to other areas of the left have not kept pace with these changes. The anti-sexist men's movement for example, is often caught in an excessive personalism that many feminists have gone beyond. The tyranny of structurelessness indicates that formal structure is necessary in democratic organisations. Too much informality leads to undemocratic practices and the emergence of elites. It makes it difficult for new people to join in. To come to a meeting and find people you do not know behaving in a very intimate way is as off-putting as coming to a meeting which is dominated by rules and standing orders. Organisations set up for particular purposes need to be run as public not as private bodies. If intimacy and informality go beyond a certain point, they create private clubs.

We join organisations not only to achieve a particular end but also to make friends. In the normal course of things there should be no conflict, but conflicts can arise. The twelve women who edited the original edition of *Our Bodies Ourselves* (the Boston Women's Health Collective) put a great deal of effort into disclosing the sort of personal information about themselves that would usually be excluded from the activities of an editorial group. They began with trepidation but gradually grew to enjoy it, eventually developing a great closeness and love for one another. They managed to do this without jeopardising the task they had set themselves.

Other groups are not so successful. I once worked for a small social-action centre in London. There were, even in this small organisation, factions, and some people got on together better than others. Since everyone was there primarily to do a job, the fact that some people did not like one another hardly mattered. Some of the workers felt differently. They thought everyone should be open with one another about their feelings, and should not cover over the hostilities that lurked below the surface. They asked, in effect, for the workers to be more intimate with one another and less instrumental. They persuaded everyone to take part in long staff meetings in which everything was to be brought into the open. These meetings were a disaster. It was not possible to heal the rifts because they were based on differences of personality. The people who got on together especially badly would never have had anything to do with each other outside work. Their relationship was not intimate, and so it was inappropriate to try and sort out their differences with intimate meetings. All that happened was that the resentments grew *worse* and the work of the organisation suffered. The pressure for intimacy was an attempt to create what Sheila Rowbotham has called a 'coercive consensus'.[5] Where intimacy is inappropriate it is bound to be coercive. Intimacy can be used as a way of dominating others.

Freud and the Victorians

The importance attached to sexuality in personal politics has a lot to do with the preference for intimate relations. Traditionally, a woman's most important relationship is thought to be her sexual relation with the man of her life. Women's liberation has encouraged more friendship between women than the female role usually allows. There is lesson for men in this: a man demands a sexual relation with a woman which will carry the weight of all his emotional needs, but men ought to distribute their emotional needs more evenly. Anything that diversifies our personal relations is to be encouraged. And yet, there *is* a great importance attaching to sexuality that hampers the development of relations of a more public and less intimate kind.

Just as the preference for intimacy in personal relations reflects preferences that have developed in the wider society, so the particular interest in sexuality reflects a corresponding evaluation of sexuality in the wider society. This changing evaluation has a lot to do with Victorian morality and the rebellion against it.

The elaborate avoidance of sex in middle-class Victorian society sprang from the ever-present awareness of it. Because sexuality is not isolated from other aspects of life, Victorian fastidiousness compelled respectable people to ignore whatever sexuality touched. Certain articles of clothing could not be so much as mentioned. Furniture had to be draped with covers so that legs could not be seen. But there was another side to Victorian life — a sexual underlife as gross as the over-life was virtuous. Prostitution flourished in city squalor. Respectable men regularly consorted with working-class prostitutes, and many had a proclivity for young girls. The age of consent was introduced largely because of the scandal of child prostitution.

The rectitude of our grandparents has been so debunked now that 'Victorian' has become a synonym for 'hypocritical', and we now consider that anything like the Victorians' attitude to sex is either dishonest or neurotic. Our attitude to sexuality has been shaped as much by our psychological assessment of the Victorians as by our moral disapproval of them. The Victorians tried to suppress sexuality, but suppression has dire consequences both for the individual and society. Psychoanalysis has taught us that. The ideas of psychoanalysis, which were resisted when Freud first expounded them, are now the commonplace of our small-talk. His *Three Essays on Sexuality* met with such opprobrium that he was shunned in the streets of Vienna. Now we can hardly discuss our lives without allusion to psychoanalysis. We subscribe implicitly to the psychoanalytic notion of sexual economy, which regards the libido as a psychic stream that will break through if it is dammed up.

The psychoanalytic revolution and our revulsion against

Victorian hypocrisy have unquestionably produced a more healthy attitude to sex. We feel less guilty about it than our grandparents did. The personal politics movement combines this attitude with a questioning of sex roles and has created great interest in sexual relations. It has, however, pursued this interest at the expense of other relations. It is not so much that there is a lack of interest in non-sexual relations: it is, rather, that intimate relations in general have been given pride of place among personal relations.

Silence in public

To give pride of place to intimacy will continue the process that has deadened public life. Intimate relations take up a great deal of personal energy, and there is a limit to the number of intimate relations we can sustain. The stress on intimacy is inspired by the desire to make people closer and more friendly, but it can only make people closer and more friendly within an ever-narrowing circle. If the only possible relations are intimate ones, and if we expend all our energy on them, non-intimate relations will suffer and public life atrophy. We need intimacy, but if we insist on making *all* relations intimate, then we will have to suffer indifference in public, the blank gaze in the railway carriage and silence in the street.

One thing intimacy demands is frankness. We live in a sincere age, and if a person is sincere it excuses many vices. A politician, for example, can be incompetent, stupid and misinformed, but people will say, 'At least he's sincere.' We think it is best to be sincere all the time. However, it is sometimes better to be less frank, in particular in non-intimate relations, which can be stifled by excessive frankness. When you ask an acquaintance how she is you do not necessarily want to know everything she is feeling at the moment. If public life is to thrive, people need to be reasonably polite to each other, but being polite rules out total frankness.

Relations between strangers cannot be conducted in the same way as relations between intimates. If there is never any dissimulation in the relations between strangers, then they are awkward and perfunctory, because everyone is fumbling for the right thing to say, or embarrassingly intimate, like the confidences of a drunk.

The lack of real sociability in modern public life shows the shortcoming of communal solutions. The anonymity of city life encourages people to form communes and to improve the quality of personal relations in collectives set up for specific tasks. Although these things have much to recommend them they do not create a truly public sociability because they are part of the private sphere. Even strict communes that deny privacy to their members (I heard of one such commune that removed all the doors in the house) touch only those within them. Personal politics ought not to confine itself to the private relations of a minority but ought to concern itself with intimate personal relations, with sociability and with public life. If it does not, it will simply give more and more attention to the private relations of fewer and fewer people, moving from the centre of political life to the margins. It will become the cult of a chosen few.

6. Only Connect

As I was delivering leaflets on a housing estate one evening, I stopped to talk to several people I knew. I met Jean and Alf Clarke,* the secretary and chairperson of the tenants' association, and talked to them about the council's forthcoming tenants' liaison meeting, and about the items we wanted to get on to the agenda. They mentioned that David Tuohy, one of the other committee members, felt that his work for the TA wasn't appreciated, and that as a result he felt isolated from the other tenants. Anne Hillier stopped me on one of the balconies and said that her husband was still giving her only £5 out of his supplementary benefit and spending the rest on himself. This had been going on for months, and she had had several interviews with the Department of Health and Social Security in an attempt to get the money paid direct to her. Kate Fraser told me she was worried about her nineteen year old son, a harmless good-natured boy, who had just gone off to live with a woman ten years older than himself.

Influencing the agenda of a tenants' liaison committee is as pure a case of social politics as you could find, since the problems of council tenants are a consequence of social conditions. In David Tuohy's feeling that he was not appreciated, the personal and the social met. He had given up a lot of his spare time trying to improve conditions on the estate and the least he could expect was that others would play their part. In Ann Hillier's problem the personal and the social combined in a different way. Her husband's irresponsibility was a problem to which there appeared to be no personal solution. Both she and her husband suffered the effects of unemployment and the indifference of the social security system. Kate Fraser's worries were thoroughly personal. She saw the older woman whom her son

---

* All names are fictitious.

had gone to live with as a temptress who had stolen a vulnerable boy. Kate worried about being abandoned, and about her son, lured into a dangerous affair. Here was a problem in personal relations into which the social did not enter. Her concerns were different from those of Anne Hillier and David Tuohy, where the personal and the social came together.

The social can impinge on friendship as it does on sexual relations. D.H. Lawrence felt subtle differences of class, and said it was these that prevented him from feeling really at home with the middle classes. He was not talking about class oppression, nor even about snobbery, but about something in the character of middle-class people that he found repellant.

> People, *personally*, have nearly always been friendly... (he said). And I have *wanted* to feel truly friendly with some, at least of my fellow men. Yet I have never quite succeeded. ...Why is there so little contact between myself and the people whom I know? Why has the contact no vital meaning? ...The answer, as far as I can see, has something to do with class. Class makes a gulf, across which all the best human flow is lost. It is not exactly the triumph of the middle classes that has made the deadness, but the triumph of the middle-class *thing*. As a man from the working class, I feel that the middle class cut off some of my vital vibration when I am with them. I admit them charming and educated and good people often enough. *But they just stop some part of me from working*. Some part has to be left out.[1]

Whatever it is that made Lawrence feel the middle classes lack passion and vibrancy it was social in origin. Whatever it was that made the working class 'narrow, but fairly deep and passionate', and the middle class 'broad and shallow and passionless',[2] it came from something in the conditions of each class. Reflecting on his personal experience, Lawrence was forced to think about social relations in order to understand it.

When we reflect on social relations we are forced to think about personal experience if we want to understand them fully. The rise in unemployment can be explained in abstract laws of social development but if you do not consider the experience of unemployment you have not really understood it. The significance of unemployment for the unemployed lies in their loss of dignity and in their having to give up things they took for granted. It lies in the rituals some unemployed men engage in, in a pathetic imitation of waged work, clocking in at the garden shed, and pottering about there from eight to five each day.

There is a connection between the social and the personal. They are distinct, but it is hard to consider one without considering how the other affects it. When we talk about some aspect of personal life, we almost always find ourselves considering social life, and when we talk about some aspect of social life we find ourselves considering the personal.

Social blindness

Not everyone recognises these connections. There is a view that society is nothing but a collection of personal relations, and that there are really no social structures distinct from them, or that the character of society is produced by the character of the individuals in it. Those who believe this say that if society is bad it is because the individuals within it are bad, or if it is good it is because individuals are good. If the behaviour of individuals deteriorates, society goes to the dogs, and if society is to improve individuals must improve first. Individuals are not formed by their society. If they appear to be it is because they are influenced by other individuals more than they ought to be, instead of being steadfast and independent.

This view is embraced by religious reformers with a social conscience, and is found in many of the religious cults that have mushroomed since the war. The Maharishi Mahesh Yogi, for example, says that if only a small number of people would practice transcendental meditation crime would disappear. It is also embraced by liberal artists who shun organised politics. Ford Madox Ford adopted a quietist anarchism, dreaming of a republic of small producers wherein all could play an equal part:

> You will say that it can never be brought about by the legislatives we have today. Certainly it can never be brought about by our present legislative procedure. It can only be brought about, let me repeat, by a changing of our own hearts. Against that no legislative can stand up.[3]

He had no understanding of the need to change the social structure.

These views can be described as social blindness. Only analysing our circumstances enables us to see social relations, because they are not in our immediate experience. But if, having been brought to the point where we are able to see this reality, we fail to do so, there is little more that thinking can do. Seeing the personal and not the social is like seeing the trees and not the wood. Social blindness makes it impossible to recognise the external influences that bear on personal life.

If we are blind to the social medium of our lives, we are unlikely to strike a balance, or establish a harmony, between our public and our private lives. Only if we see the way that the social impinges on the personal (and vice versa) can we appreciate the need to balance the private and the public. Otherwise they exist in a condition of irremediable separation and difference. The need to achieve the balance is not, however, one that everyone feels, only those who have an active public life. The majority of people, excluded from social power and influence, are confined to a more-or-less private existence. Their public lives are lives not of politics, but of public places and urban space, an arena that is now almost completely devoid of personal intercourse. Although the question of balance does not affect everyone directly, it is relevant to socialism. For socialism has to increase participation in politics, thereby opening up public life to greater numbers of people.

Solidarity and collective action have such strong working-class connotations that it is easy to forget they are habits as natural to the bourgeoisie as to the working class. In the middle-class hand-wringing over collective action by workers, the collective action of the upper class is frequently overlooked. Even Adam Smith recognised that combinations, which employers tried to prevent when workers first began to form them in the eighteenth century, were more common among the employing class than they were among the working class. 'We seldom, indeed, hear of this combination,' said Smith, 'because it is the usual, and one may say, the natural state of things which nobody ever hears of.'[4] And few who say trade unions are too powerful today spare a thought for the plethora of employers' unions — from The Confederation of British Industry to the Cake and Biscuit Alliance.

The personal lives of ruling-class individuals are so palpably connected with social forces that one might imagine individualism to be alien to them. The vistas opened by their public lives ought to show the connections, yet one frequently discovers amongst them a curious social blindness. Failing to connect, the bourgeois individual often imagines that high office or public renown are won purely by personal effort and ability. Failing to connect, he often regards his income and what he does with it as a private matter, even though it comes from the social relations which he is part of. And failing to connect, he may believe that the way he behaves in public life has little to do with the way he behaves in private.

Public and private morals

From time to time a scandal is uncovered, and a public figure is imprisoned or shunned. He may have corrupted those with influence, defrauded gullible victims, or compromised himself in some way or another. Whether his actions were technical transgressions or brought ruin to many, he acted dishonestly or immorally in public. Such was the Profumo scandal, in which a minister who had access to defence secrets associated with prostitutes who had Russian clients. Such was the Stonehouse scandal, in which an MP faked his death to evade charges of fraud. Such was the Poulson scandal in which a local councillor took bribes from a builder. If a person fails to connect, his wrongdoing in public does not necessarily tell us a great deal about his private morals. People are quite capable of dividing up their lives so that they behave badly in public and well in private. Similarly, a politician who advocates harmful social policies may be considerate in his face-to-face contacts.

While canvassing in the 1979 British general election, Sir Keith Joseph, for example, showed a concern for voters at odds with the way in which he was going to treat them once he got into office. He found difficulty in canvassing because he was reluctant to disturb the voters! The local candidate thought it might be a good idea to visit a local supermarket, presumably in the hope of interrupting a few potential supporters, but Sir Keith demurred. 'Do you think it's proper to go in?' 'I do try and avoid places with customers in.'[5]

The vices of left-wing males also spring from a failure to connect. The businessman and the bourgeois politician may be opportunist in public but in private may show a better side. The left-wing male, by contrast, adheres to a pure political morality yet he has often proved to be selfish in private. His vice comes from attaching a disproportionate importance to social politics. An altruist when it comes to those living thousands of miles away, in Vietnam or Latin America, he is an egotist at home. Capable of trenchant analysis of the political scene, he is obtuse when it comes to personal relations: 'His roots are with the rootless. That's where he wants to be; He will die with total strangers, But he will not live with me.'[6]

Social determinism

There is the opposite view that the personal is not autonomous at all, which is just as mistaken in its way. It denies that personal life is really distinct from social life, and holds that the personal is all but completely determined by the social. Marxism is for socialists the most important political version of this view, and since so many of the ideas of marxism run counter to the ideas of personal politics it is necessary to take marxism into consideration here.

In the hands of its less imaginative interpreters marxism has been turned into a bleak social determinism, which compares the forces of society to the pitiless forces of nature. This marxism squeezes out the individual, discarding her wishes in favour of social forces. Bykhovsky, a Soviet hack of exceptional wooden-headedness, writes of personal life in these hard words: 'What makes up the individual and his inner world, his needs, inclinations, propensities, views, concepts, convictions, habits, hopes and feelings is all developed, moulded and determined by his social environment.'[7] He grinds out the doctrine in prose reminiscent of the legal documents that give long lists of alternatives in order that nothing should escape their edict. He is not slow to point out the political implications of these words. In the Soviet Union it is futile to pit subjective wishes, personal opinions, the ideal of self-development, or political protest against the might of society, for the individual is nothing and society everything.

The extreme determinism one finds in Soviet marxism probably appears strange to those accustomed to western marxism, which has learnt from Marx's early writings the importance of subjectivity and individuality. Marxists are beginning to learn from the women's movement as well, and to consider those areas of life that have for long been dismissed as non-political. And yet, despite those marxists who recognise the importance of subjectivity and the personal, the tendency to submerge them beneath the social and the objective is there in all marxism.

There is an ambivalence in marxism concerning the relation between the personal and the social. The part played in social change by objective laws of history and the part played by human will and consciousness hang in the balance. Marx strove to connect the personal and the social, the objective and the subjective. He strove to connect without submerging either one or the other. He rejected French materialism and German idealism because they were both one-sided, and he combined elements of each in his historical materialism. From French materialism he took the doctrine that the material world determines consciousness, and from German idealism he took the doctrine that human consciousness plays a creative role in history. He developed a theory of society which held that subjective and objective were united in human activity. Human activity was subjective, in that the consciousness of individuals entered into it, and objective, in that it had effect in the world. Out of the actions of individuals, each pursuing their personal ends, emerge objective social relations which in turn determine the actions of individuals. Individual and society, subjectivity and objectivity, acted and reacted on each other.

Minds that are accustomed to choosing between simple alternatives find this theory hard to grasp. Western thought has always chosen between alternatives and opposites; the rule of 'either/or' is supreme. It is perhaps inevitable that Marx's historical materialism, which flouts this rule, should set up a tension in the minds of all who try to grasp it. In western thought there is a desire to make either one side or the other supreme: either the subjective or the objective; either the personal or the social. Marx himself was not free from this tension, and that is why he tended to come down on one side. Marxism, from Marx's own time, submerged the personal and subjective beneath the social and objective.

The tension appears, for example, in Marx's theory of consciousness. 'It is not consciousness that determines life,' he says, 'but life that determines consciousness.'[8] This appears unequivocal enough. Yet in the same work as this sentence appears, the matter is expressed rather differently: 'Circumstances make men just as much as men make circumstances.'[9] The 'circumstances' that men make are a part of their 'life', and the men who make circumstances are conscious. Their ideas and feelings, their observations and superstitions — in a word, their consciousness — contributes to the making of circumstances. Consciousness, therefore, *does* determine life. Marx may have stated the matter uncompromisingly, but he did not mean it quite as unequivocally as he appears to at first.

By his late fifties Marx had resolved the tension in his own mind by emphasising the determination of the individual by the social, and the determination of consciousness by objective conditions. He began to be attracted to the positivist philosophy then fashionable in intellectual circles.[10] Positivism was uncompromisingly objectivistic in its view of society. The idea of social laws became, in Marx's mind, more important than the idea of the creativity of human action. The positivistic version of marxism was set out by Engels, with Marx's approval, in *Anti-Dühring*, a work that was to have a wide circulation in the socialist movement, and a considerable influence on socialist thought. *Anti-Dühring* is the first treatise on dialectical materialism, a philosophy in which natural and social laws are supreme, and in which the subjective and the personal are of subordinate importance.

In the debate within marxism over the 'Young Marx' and the 'Old Marx', the main point at issue is whether there was a significant change in Marx's outlook between the time when he tried to transcend French materialism and German idealism and the time when he began to show an interest in positivism, between the Marx of the *Economic and Philosophical Manuscripts* and the Marx of *Capital*. I believe that in talking of the Young Marx and the Old Marx it is easy to exaggerate whatever change in outlook there may have been. One can find the ideas of the *Economic and Philosophical Manuscripts* buried beneath the economic algebra of *Capital*. The idea of alienation, for example, so characteristic of the Young Marx, appears repeatedly in the writings of the Old Marx. Marx's outlook was constant: the humanism of his early years remained, yet the social determinism of his late years was already there at the beginning, even in his theory of alienation.

According to this theory, the worker is in a society

dominated by private property, alienated from the products of her labour, from her labour itself, and from the human essence. Marx believed alienation from the human essence to be the most terrible consequence of private property. He believed that in productive activity lay the essence of the human species, the quality that distinguished human beings from beasts. The effect of private property was to make productive activity alien to the worker. The alienated worker treats production as merely the means by which she gains her livelihood, rather than as an expression of her humanity. In alienation, the human essence becomes merely a means to the personal existence of individuals. In treating the social relations of production as the mere means to personal existence, rather than as the essence of her humanity, the worker shows the deep rupture in human nature under private property.

For Marx, the belief that social relations are only means to an end is a product of humanity's alienation from itself, and the idea that the essence of human life is to be found in personal rather than social relations is an indictment of capitalist society. Marx's theory, right from the early years is hostile to the personal. The tendency to submerge the personal under the social is not a product of his later inclination to positivism. It is present in his youthful theories.

Continuous excursions

Marxism does more than connect. It explains away, absorbs, reduces and submerges the personal. This is the consequence of social determinism, which denies the autonomy of personal life and insists on its subservience to social relations. In practice too, the tendency of marxism has been to reduce and submerge the personal. In marxist practice, social politics is always more important than personal politics, and social life is always more important than personal life.

Marxist social determinism is found even among those who are not marxists. It is found among feminists and among others committed to personal politics. The attempt to connect the social and the personal often submerges the personal under the social, and those who make the attempt are often influenced by the marxist outlook more than they realise. There is in feminism, for all its stress on the personal and subjective, a tendency to social determinism. The passage I quoted in Chapter 2 tended very strongly to social determinism. It spoke of 'the illusion that a woman's relationship with her man is a matter of interplay between two unique personalities', and insisted that, on the contrary, 'every such relationship is a class relationship'.[11] It subjected sexual relations to the rule of 'either/or': it claimed that a relationship must be *either* social *or* personal, and concluded that, since sexual relations are social, they cannot be personal.

The idea that we should fuse the personal and the social is an expression of social determinism. Personal politics made the attempt to connect, but it did not rest content: it then tried to submerge. It is ironical that in personal politics we should find the same sort of social determinism that we find in marxism, since personal politics was supposed to be a radical break with marxist ideology. In many respects it is, but marxism has become so influential that it has encouraged a way of looking at the world which is occasionally shared even by those who reject it.

Two pictures hang above my desk. One is a photograph of Marx taken in the 1870s as he was approaching his sixtieth year. It shows a proud man with a head like Zeus, a high-domed brow, and a grizzled beard. His features are blunt and pugnacious, his moustache is still thick and black, his hand is thrust carelessly into a plain, black coat. It shows a man who has achieved nearly all he will achieve. The other picture I have is William Blake's drawing of *The Reunion of the Soul and the Body*. It shows a figure bursting joyously from the grave as all around him is consumed in fire. Another figure descends through the smoke to clasp his neck in an embrace. To me these disparate images represent a common theme — the theme of connection. In his early work Marx sought, in a sense, the reunion of the soul and the body. He repudiated the Young Hegelians, who snapped their fingers at material forces, and he also repudiated the mechanical materialists, who conceived of reality only as objects, not subjectively. In his early work he spoke of reality as 'human sensuous activity'. Human sensuous activity unites the soul and the body.

Only connect, but do not submerge — that should be our task. 'Only connect' is a phrase of E.M. Forster's. In *Howards End*, from which the phrase is taken, his connection of the personal and social is at its most felicitous.

The businessman who assumes that this life is everything and the mystic who asserts that it is nothing, fail, on this side and on that, to hit the truth. 'Yes, I see, dear; it's about halfway between,' Aunt Juley had hazarded in earlier years. No; truth, being alive, was not halfway between anything. It was only to be found by continuous excursions into either realm, and though proportion is the final secret, to espouse it at the outset is to ensure sterility.[12]

We do not have to choose between personal life and politics, between a public life and a private life. In explaining the nature of the personal we do not have to adopt either an individualist or a collectivist view. We do not have to come down either on the side of the subjective or the objective. We have to avoid all one-sidedness and fanaticism, and make continuous excursions into either realm.

7. Individualism and Personal Autonomy

Some have said that personal politics is individualistic because it stresses the subjective experience of individuals. Critics of personal politics often say that feminism is bourgeois because many feminists are in white-collar jobs or the professions. All-in-all, say these critics, personal politics reeks of bourgeois individualism.

In a sense personal politics *is* individualistic. It makes changes in individuals' lives the touchstone of social progress. It urges individuals to take control over their own lives. But it is not bourgeois, nor does it make the same mistakes as the victims of social blindness.

Personal politics is quite different from the individualism of nineteenth century liberals, with their belief in *laissez faire* and economic competition. A look at the history of the concept of individualism will help us to understand the difference.

People commonly see individualism emerging alongside capitalism in the seventeenth century, but the concept itself is of more recent origin. It arose in France in the aftermath of the Revolution, and was first used by French monarchists and Catholics to condemn the ascendancy of private judgement and the dissolution of traditional hierarchy. In 1820 the monarchist de Maistre spoke of 'this deep and frightening division of minds, this infinite fragmentation of all doctrines, political protestantism carried to the most ultimate individualism'.[1] Lammenais deprecated the individualism 'which destroys the very idea of obedience and duty, thereby destroying both power and law; and what then remains but a terrifying confusion of interest, passions and diverse opinions'.[2] The philosophy of the Enlightenment had, in the opinion of these French conservatives, subverted the fixed order of the estates, the family, the church and the monarchy, and had unleashed upon society a turmoil of individual wills. Social harmony, they held, depended on the subordination of personal judgement to doctrinal authority and on the restriction of individuals to their proper station in life.

Although the word was invented by reactionaries it was soon taken up by socialists, who used it to describe disorder of bourgeois society. The influence of French socialism was so great that this usage has passed into the modern socialist vocabulary. Some French socialists, however, recognised that individualism meant not only a war of wills but also the full development of individuals, and they held that individualism in the latter sense could be achieved only under socialism. Louis Blanc contrasted individualism with fraternity: individualism was a rebellion against traditional authority and therefore contributed to human freedom, but it was incomplete if it did not pass into fraternity. Fraternity transcended individualism, retaining its virtues and eliminating its vices, and it made individual freedom possible without competition and selfishness. Fourier denied that there was any conflict between socialism and individualism, and Jaurès held that 'socialism is the logical completion of individualism'.[3]

From the first, the word 'individualism' has had subtle nuances, implying on the one hand the ruthless pursuit of individual self-interest, and on the other the self-development of individuals. It is important to appreciate these nuances and to recognise that individualism does not always mean competitiveness.

Many words begin life as terms of abuse, only to be embraced by the very people they abuse. 'Quaker', for example, was first used to mock the tremulous worship of the Society of Friends, and 'Suffragette' was first used condescendingly to describe female suffragists. Friends came to call themselves Quakers and suffragists suffragettes. 'Individualism', first used to dismiss revolutionaries, now describes several coherent philosophies of the individual: respect for the individual, a belief in personal autonomy, and the doctrine of economic competition. They should not be equated: indeed the first two are incompatible with the third.

Respect for individuals

In a political context, respect for individuals means that the welfare and growth of individuals, rather than the efficiency of organisations or the glory of leaders, should be the final goal. Society, social organisations and politics are only means to this end, not ends in themselves. Moral philosophers have frequently insisted that the only valid ends are individuals. Marx, despite his theory that social relations are the human essence, was undoubtedly an individualist in this sense. He hated capitalism because it deformed human beings, and he envisaged communism as a state of society in which individuals no longer had to labour for the wealth of a few, but had the opportunity to pursue their own ends. Feminists have a similar respect for individuals. They condemn patriarchy because it treats women as means towards the wellbeing of men, rather than as ends in themselves, and as sexual objects, rather than subjects with their own desires.

It is, however, not always easy to apply this doctrine consistently. Whatever the goal of political action, all political organisations must have intermediate goals. Intermediate goals, such as electoral success, the building of an organisation, or the success of a campaign, may require that one treats individuals instrumentally for the while. Disciplined revolutionary organisations often burn up recruits in frantic activity, and parliamentary organisations often treat voters as ballot fodder. In the rough-and-tumble of strike action it is not always possible to be considerate with strike-breakers. The organisation of a socialist society itself raises problems concerning respect for individuals and their ends. The wellbeing of all calls for a planned economy, but economic planning is restrictive. For example, there is a conflict between the need to plan the labour force, and therefore the birth-rate, and the right of women to control their own fertility.

Some people have concluded from the difficulty of applying the principle of respect for individuals that it should be abandoned and that collective welfare is a worthier end. The collectivity whose welfare is aimed at may be the state, the nation or the working class, or something more general, such as the people, or something more specific, such as the particular party which happens to be in power.

There are two good reasons why we should not abandon the principle of respect for individuals. The first is that the practical problems encountered in applying it do not necessarily amount to a conflict between the wellbeing of individuals and the welfare of a collectivity, and the second is that the consequences of abandoning it may be very serious.

Take the conflict between the need to plan the labour force and women's right to control their fertility. Both these things boil down to the principle of respect for individuals. The welfare of individuals requires some degree of social and economic planning, since the free working of the market actually prevents the wellbeing of a large number of individuals in favour of the luxury of a few. Some planning of the labour force is necessary if we want to avoid unemployment, with its bad effect on workers, and a shortage of suitable skills, with its bad effect on consumers; the point about these bad effects is that they are felt as a loss of wellbeing by individuals. There are, of course, social as well as personal consequences (such as the recent rioting in British cities) but these social consequencs only come about when the malaise felt by individuals erupts and becomes visible on a large scale, or enters into the social structure. Similarly, restrictions on women's freedom in matters of conception, contraception and abortion is undesirable because it has a bad effect on individual women. This conflict is therefore a conflict between the wellbeing of different individuals rather than between the wellbeing of individuals and the welfare of a collectivity; or rather it is a conflict between the different ends that any individual may have, since workers, consumers and women are not separate groups of people, and the same person is simultaneously worker, consumer and woman.

Conflicts of ends are inevitable to some extent; thus the idea that we should respect individuals may lead to conflict if it involves respect for conflicting ends. Unfortunately, the idea that all conflicts arise from class conflict is so current on the left that many socialists find it hard to accept that there may be genuine conflicts that have nothing to do with class — conflicts between individuals and conflicts among the ends desired by one individual. If all such conflicts *were* attributable to the existence of classes, then a collectivist approach might get round them; since they are not, it only masks those that are individual in nature.

The second reason why we should not abandon respect for individuals is that it is a strong defence against authoritarian and elitist politics. As soon as one ceases to make individual wellbeing the ultimate end of political action one makes it possible to sacrifice the tangible benefits for individuals to intangible collective ends, such as the neatness of social planning or the glory of a nation. It also makes it possible to sacrifice the wellbeing of the majority to the power of a minority. Authoritarian governments have often stated quite explicitly that they sacrifice the wellbeing of individuals to the welfare of the collectivity.

Individualism in the sense of respect for individuals is therefore a strong defence of libertarianism.

Personal autonomy

Respect for individuals is connected with the ideal of personal autonomy, which means the power to determine and pursue one's own goals in life. Respect for individuals would mean very little if individuals were denied this power of self-determination. Personal autonomy requires that you should be able to discriminate between alternative courses of action, and to follow your chosen course. Three conditions have to be met before one can be said to act autonomously. First, one's choices have to be conscious; second, they have to be informed; third, one has to be able to do what one has chosen. A prisoner has no autonomy because the choice between imprisonment and liberty is not one she has the capacity to carry out. Other cases are less straightforward. For example, a woman brought up in a traditional way, and caught in a restrictive marriage, is not powerless in the sense that a prisoner is, yet her constraints are such that she has little autonomy.

Autonomy means freedom. Even in the absence of external restraints one may be unfree, for there are inner restraints as well. Chronic indecision, for example, prevents some people from achieving much in their lives, because they never know what they want, or never want anything long enough to get it before changing their minds. Feelings of guilt may also paralyse action, always placing an individual's wishes, preferences and intentions before an invisible judge. The fact that we may be constrained by psychological forces makes it clear that there are obstacles to autonomy other than the obvious social and political ones.

Inner restraints often come from our past, and though we cannot change the past we can understand what has shaped us and we can free ourselves from its influence. Sometimes we can remove these inner restraints by reflection or an effort of will. Sometimes we cannot do so without some sort of psychotherapy.

Sheila Rowbotham has written of the way she used to avoid theories of organisation, and how she uncovered the cause of her inhibition. She thought about the influence her dead father still exerted over her, and how it made her afraid of theory. 'I saw obscurely that unless I could spiritually meet my own father person to person,' she says, 'I would continue to simply react against and oppose all forms of authority rather than confront and contest them in the open.'[4] Through talking to other women about their feelings towards their fathers, she managed to confront her own feelings. Unwinding her fears in this way enabled her to overcome the feeling of dread that theories of organisation had always inspired in her. In uncovering past causes in this way, one moves a step away from their influence and ceases to be the person one was.

Self-development

This possibility of becoming a new person indicates an important aspect of autonomy, that is, self-development. Self-development is the realisation of human possibilities. A person who acts out of habit, and thereby fails to achieve autonomy, fails to realise her potential for growth and change.

Personal change in itself does not amount to self-development, and may actually hinder it. Individuals may be forced to change as a result of external pressure. They may be pressurised into conforming, or they may be expected to adjust their way of life by a political or religious group. Religious cults, such as Scientology, EST, and the Moonies make recruits change their personalities and they have all developed sophisticated techniques for securing it. Friends and relatives of those who have joined cult organisations have reported very radical changes in them. The changes wrought by membership of fanatical political organisations may not be as far-reaching as those wrought by religious cults, but they are comparable. The organisation swamps the individual and controls her thoughts and deeds. We should even regard consciousness-raising with caution since it can be used to secure political conformity rather than personal development.

Autonomy and the realisation of personal goals demands assertiveness and self-confidence. We cannot achieve much in our lives if we are always modest and self-effacing. All of us, and women especially, have been brought up to make a virtue of humility, and the women's movement has been quick to see how important it is to be assertive. It is now possible to take courses in assertiveness training, and this is all to the good. These courses show that assertiveness is not the same as aggressiveness, and that in personal relations aggressiveness betrays a lack of assertiveness. Habitually unassertive people deny themselves in little things and fail to resist little encroachments on their autonomy, until a point is reached when they explode in anger. Anger and aggression often fail to achieve what they want because they dissipate their energy in heated emotional displays.

Competitive individualism

The sort of individualism I have been describing is often confused with competitive individualism, and is thrown out with it. All forms of individualism are condemned indiscriminately. From time to time one finds this indiscriminate anti-individualism in collective organisations where self-assertiveness, personal judgements, the nurturing of individual abilities or dissent from the collective consensus are discouraged as competitive. But these kinds of individualism are not competitive at all.

Competitive individualism — the capitalist doctrine of unfettered economic competition — embraces the following principles: the best interests of society as a whole are served if individuals pursue their own private interests; material inequality is a good thing because the prospect of exceptional rewards is the only guarantee of exceptional achievement; the market is the best social regulator and permits greater individual freedom than economic planning; the activities of government should be limited as far as possible; and collective bodies should be discouraged because they restrict economic activity.

Several of these principles were first expounded in the seventeenth century by political theorists like Hobbes and Locke, and they found their fullest expression in the views of the Manchester school in the nineteenth century. Milton Friedman is their most passionate publicist today, and his role as the guru of right-wing governments has elevated him from the obscurity of the American academic community to the stardom of a television series. This is *real* bourgeois individualism. Bourgeois individualists pay lipservice to the other sorts of individualism, we know that well enough. But that is not the important thing. It does not matter what they *say*. What counts is that a regime of unfettered competition cannot respect individuals and cannot allow them autonomy. We should not be misled by high-sounding phrases and good intentions. Inequality, competition, and self aggrandisement prevent large numbers of people from leading the lives they want to lead. Capitalist society treats people as means rather than ends.

The fact that these distinct varieties of individualism are historically connected persuades some that they are inseparable. Capitalism undid the communal ties that bound individuals together, and weakened the traditional groups of which they were part. The protective organisation of the craft guilds was dissolved in the growth of capitalistic production. Rural communities where the duties of the poor had been balanced by the responsibilities of the rich were gradually replaced by communities in which individuals had to fend for themselves. In seventeenth century England the new economic individualism, which preached attention to one's private interests, came into conflict with the ideal of Christian charity, which preached succour to the distressed. The rise of a new gentry in the English village created turbulent social conflicts. The traditional bonds of a customary society were broken, and ideas about individuality started to grow. Where previously the individual was merged into the community there grew up the idea that the individual might have goals of her own distinct from communal goals. Various cultural changes attested to this growth of individuality out of communal unity. In art the self-portrait emerged. In everyday life a better type of mirror allowed more contemplation of one's own image. In the home separate chairs took the place of long benches. In religion the idea of personal conscience eroded the authority of the church. In Renaissance Italy, whose trading ports and cities were the cradle of mercantile capitalism, the notion of the all-round man furnished the ideal of personal development.

Yet personal development was possible only for a small number of men, and it has been so ever since. The upper classes provide many examples of men who have led full and satisfying lives. Increasing material equality has made a rounded life possible for a larger number, but for many it still remains impossible. So too does individuality, in the sense of developing personal differences. Indeed, modern capitalism has created a society increasingly undifferentiated. We live in the world of the assembly line, the supermarket and the package holiday.

Faced with the unfulfilled ideals of individualism, some people adopt a curious attitude towards them. The ideals have been hollow under capitalism, they say, therefore we will have none of them; individualism in all its forms is a capitalist creation, so socialists must reject it; the ideas of personal autonomy, self-development and economic competition are bourgeois to the core, so out with them all. Saying this is like saying that industry is a capitalist product, therefore we should go back to the horse-plough, or that science is a capitalist product, therefore we should go back to superstition. It would be more sensible to recognise that the reason why individualism is an unfulfilled ideal is that it actually subverts capitalism and points the way towards a socialist society.

The fact that personal development has been possible for those with wealth shows its incompatibility with bourgeois individualism. The inequality praised by bourgeois individualists allows personal development to only a few. If it is to become possible for everybody, then there must be greater material equality. Without a reasonable standard of living one has little opportunity to develop because one's energies have to be put into sustaining life.

Recent studies of poverty have moved away from definitions in terms of absolute wealth towards a definition in terms of relative wealth. They define poverty as a condition in which a people are, by virtue of their low standard of living, cut off from the life of those around them. Poverty in industrial societies excludes people from activities in which other people around them engage. If someone cannot afford to travel, while those around her can, she leads a life which is not only materially impoverished, but socially impoverished as well. Material inequality therefore means fewer opportunities for social activities, and therefore fewer opportunities for personal development.

Where there is material inequality one always finds political inequality. In any society, the richer one is the more one is able to influence the course of events. The rich have a greater chance of getting public office, and if they do not get it themselves a greater chance of influencing those who do. The poorer one is, the less likely it is that one will take part in politics or be able to influence it. This is partly because money bestows free time and partly because people with money are more likely to mix in the 'right' circles than those without it.

Those who defend material inequality say that in a democracy everyone is politically equal because everyone can vote. This argument shows a very limited understanding of democracy and considerable naivety about the way government works. Between elections every government is influenced by public reaction and by effective pressure groups. It is in the nature of things that those who are rich are better able to lobby than those who are poor. Real democracy not only gives the vote but also makes it possible for everyone to share power. It puts everyone on an equal footing as far as influencing decisions is concerned, and therefore it requires that everyone should have equal wealth.

Personal autonomy is not possible for everyone without material equality because one cannot pursue one's goals on the same terms as others if one does not share power on equal terms, and one cannot share power on equal terms if one does not have an equal share of wealth. The material inequality preached by competitive individualists is therefore incompatible with one of the basic principles of individualism. Respect for individuals is also incompatible with competitive individualism. It is inconsistent to claim that all individuals deserve respect, yet that some should be rich and some poor, or to claim that all individuals should be treated as ends, yet that some should exploit or ruin others.

Personal development is achieved not just by accumulating material goods, which the necessity of material equality may suggest, but through activity as well. That is why engaging in social activities with other people is so important. Full self-development comes not only through recreational activities, important as they are, but also through joining with others in communal, political and economic life. That is another reason why bourgeois individualism is incompatible with individualism in the sense of self-development: bourgeois individualism insists that individuals seek their own welfare in competition with others, rather than through co-operation, and it deprecates any form of collectivism. Joining with others in the life of society calls for collective endeavour and collective organisation. Bourgeois individualists regard collective activity as oppressive and restrictive, but it has the potential to enrich our lives.

The confusion about individualism has been very damaging, and it has, perhaps, been nowhere so damaging as in the personal politics movement. For personal politics is, as I have said, individualistic. The confused notions of individualism that abound have led to worries that need not exist. I have known people berated for their individualism who then withdrew from groups with a feeling of disquiet they could not put their finger on. They felt that the personal values they advocated were right, they felt it was necessary to find personal solutions, they felt that the individual did not have to get lost in a coercive consensus, but they also felt they had aligned themselves unwittingly with bourgeois ideology. They certainly did not agree with Milton Friedman that social inequality should be preserved — but didn't their defence of personal solutions put them in the same camp? They certainly did not agree with Mrs Thatcher that everyone ought to fend for themselves — but didn't their defence of personal initiative put them on the same side? Were they individualists or were they not? And if they were individualists, didn't that mean they were bourgeois?

The positive ideals of individualism clash with the capitalist variety and call for more co-operation than capitalism permits. Individualism conflicts with neither socialism nor feminism. If we fail to see this, and if we imagine there is some conflict between individualism and collectivism, then we betray the very ideals we should be fighting for. The ideals at the heart of socialism and feminism should bend politics towards the person, not the person towards politics. Personal politics should overcome the conflict between collectivism and individualism. It should base itself on personal values, personal solutions and resistance to the coercive consensus. Otherwise it simply carries forward the values of the assembly line, the supermarket and the package holiday.

8. Capitalism, the Family and Personal Life

When I began thinking about this book I looked around bookships and libraries to see what other people had written about the personal and the political. I found many books on feminism, I read papers from the gay movement and the anti-sexist men's movement, I found 'the personal is political' repeated many times, but I could not find what I was looking for. No-one seemed to deal with the issues raised by 'the personal is political'. No-one seemed to deal with the nature of personal life and politics or with the nature of public life and privacy.

Some books looked hopeful. There was Sara Evans's *Personal Politics*, which seemed as if it might answer my questions. It turned out to be the best account yet written about the origins of the women's movement in the sixties, but not what I wanted. Then there was Marx, who, like all social philosophers, considered the question of the individual and society, consciousness and history, and I learnt a lot from him. But having asserted that society is based as much on relations between the sexes as on economic relations, he promptly forgot it and had little to say about them.[1] I also learnt a lot from Reich, who did consider relations between the sexes but Reich wrote before 'the personal is political' was coined, and could not address himself to the problems it raised.

Capitalism, the Family and Personal Life looked very promising indeed. Written by Eli Zaretsky, and first published in 1973, it took up questions of the family and the economy, subjectivity and society, the inner and the outer worlds, individualism and personal life. Zaretsky did something interesting. He put these questions in a historical setting. He made me realise that we need to understand the history of personal life if we are to understand the nature of personal life.

I welcomed Zaretsky's book, but it was not what I was looking for either. Zaretsky is a marxist and his enthusiasm for personal politics is muted; he is a social determinist and he thinks personal life is not really distinct from social life; he muddles up different things. In the end his effort to understand personal life is unsuccessful because he never gets a clear idea of what it is.

Feminists — Kate Millett, Shulamith Firestone and Juliet Mitchell — have, he says, been right to show how the personal/political division corresponds to the family/work division. (You must bear in mind that Zaretsky often says 'political' when he means 'social'.) Women stay at home and lead a private life, while men go to work and lead a public life. Social politics becomes a male preserve and women are excluded. But, says Zaretsky, feminists fail to understand that these divisions came about not because of male supremacy, which he admits is ancient, but because capitalism changed the social and sexual division of labour. Home and workplace were once one place; capitalism reorganised production and made them two places. If we do not understand these historical changes, he says, we will never understand the personal/political division. If we do not understand the division, we can never heal it. In order to understand it and to heal it we need a unified marxist theory which embraces family and society, sexual relations and economic relations, personal and political, inner and outer worlds.

The split

In pre-capitalist society, says Zaretsky, the family was responsible not only for the functions it has today, but also for productive work. In feudal society the peasant family worked together on the lands owned by their lord, then, with the dissolution of feudal relations, the peasant family assumed a new importance as a unit of production. Extricating themselves from feudal bondage, peasants became tenants or landowners in their own right, and every member of the family, men and women, old and young, worked the family plot together. Whereas goods such as clothes, furniture or household utensils had hitherto been made by people for their own use, or the use of their near neighbours, artisans now set up workshops to produce for a larger market. In these workshops, as on the peasant holdings, the members of the family all had a part to play. Up to the nineteenth century, 'there was scarcely a division *between* the family and the world of commodity production,' and society 'was overwhelmingly composed of family units based upon widely dispersed, individually owned productive property'.[2] Moreover, the family in early capitalist society was not a small two-generation family like the modern family: it was 'a complicated economic enterprise that included not only children and relatives but servants, apprentices, and journeymen from different social classes' as well.[3]

Modern industry destroyed this extended family which lived where it worked. With the advent of modern industrial production people no longer earned their living (whether as agricultural or manufacturing workers) from their own property, but worked at others' property, which took them away from their homes. At first whole families went to a common workshop, and there the father's authority, which had gone unchallenged in the house, was undermined by the authority of the master. Later, the family at work was split up, and then, during the course of the nineteenth century women and children were excluded from factory work. Journeymen and apprentices had been driven from the home workshop to a factory, and in similar fashion the master moved from the home to an office. The Victorian bourgeois moved back and forth between the world of industry or commerce and the world of the family where his wife would be waiting for him. Thus there grew a distinct sphere of family life associated with women. In the twentieth century the same process occurred among the working class. The factory system had created a propertyless proletariat, but as living standards rose a home life similar to that of the middle class became possible for workers. In its turn the working-class family also became a haven from waged work.

As home and work were torn apart, and as women became bound to the family, so people began to see their personal life as something that attached to the family and not to their work. Personal life assumed an importance it had never had before — indeed, according to Zaretsky, personal life did not exist until it was brought into being by this division of home and work. The distinguishing feature of personal life was its subjectivity, and modern life, where the personal is all-important, is obsessed with the subjective.

Capitalism created a harsh world of exploitation. 'In opposition to this harsh world that no individual could hope to affect the modern world of subjectivity was created.'[4] People have become more and more obsessed with subjective things in the course of this century and have lost all sense of the connection between their personal lives and the wider society. Personal experience alone is the source of meaning in their lives, and they view personal life as 'an entirely subjective phenomenon having meaning only for the individual.'[5] Cults and foibles of all kinds have flourished on this fertile ground: utopianism, existentialism, bohemianism, hippy culture, psychoanalysis, communitarianism, sexual freedom and radical feminism. All these movements and theories attempt to solve personal problems in a private way. Such attempts are doomed to failure, says Zaretsky. Only by diffusing our personal needs through society, and especially through work, can we hope to solve the personal problems that face us in the modern world. Only socialism can integrate the personal and the political. Under socialism the personal will no longer be a sphere separate from the rest of society, but neither will our lives be dominated by relations of production as they are now.

Zaretsky's book has many virtues. First, in trying to show the relation between the personal and the social he has gone to the heart of the problem. Second, he draws a finely-shaded picture of women's position in society, showing how it has changed over the years. Third, he has a conception of the economy that makes impossible the crudities and oversimplifications of economism. By the economy he means the entire production of material life, including sexual reproduction, the care of children, home life and health care. By including gender relations within the economy he avoids the common mistakes of thinking that gender relations are less important than economic life. For Zaretsky, gender relations are part of the foundation of society, and are of comparable importance to relations of production. He recognises that any alteration of gender relations is quite as fundamental as any alteration of relations of production. Fourth, he recognises that the flight into subjectivity embodies contradictions which are potentially disruptive. Modern capitalism has alienated people from work and social life, and has made them turn to their family and their personal relations for all their satisfaction. In doing so they put an enormous a strain on their personal life, and demand from it a satisfaction it cannot provide. Ultimately people are bound to realise this and to turn outward and change their social conditions. And finally, he understands the need to make connections, and deprecates both apolitical personalism and impersonal politics.

Despite its virtues, however, Zaretsky's book is vitiated by its lack of clarity about the nature of personal life. He recognises that personal life is important and that socialists should attend to it more closely than many of them have done in the past, but he does not recognise the difference between personal life and social life. He fails to see that the subjectivity, which he believes 'rose' during a particular epoch, is the essence of the personal and not a delusion. Failing to distinguish properly between the personal and the social he fails to distinguish properly between personal politics and social politics. Politics, as Zaretsky understands it, is really only about society, he has nothing to say about the political processes we find in personal relations. Politics and the social get confused as well — indeed, we see in this book all the confusions I mentioned in the first two chapters. Zaretsky's hesitations about feminist politics are very much the result of his confusions. The women's liberation movement, he says, is deficient because 'the focus on the family and personal relations has proved an insufficient basis for a political movement'.[6] By a political movement, of course, he means a movement of social politics, not a movement of personal politics.

Zaretsky's intention are plain. He wants to warn us of the danger of turning inwards and of ignoring social relations and public life. He is right to warn us, but he does not understand where the danger comes from. It comes not from personal politics as such, but from the cultivation of intimate personal relations at the expense of non-intimate ones. Zaretsky does not see this because he does not distinguish between social relations and public life, or between intimate and non-intimate personal relations. Intimate personal relations are those we form in private life; in public we form less intimate relations, but they are still personal. Zaretsky thinks the only way to avoid the dangers of introspection is to put society above personal life. For him we are faced with a simple choice: subjectivism or society. Fortunately the choice is not so simple, and personal relations are sufficiently varied for us to lead a public life without abandoning them.

Subjectivity

Zaretsky has a great deal to say about subjectivity, but he does not really clarify what it is. When he talks about the search for self-fulfilment in modern society, he says 'The distinguishing character of this search is its subjectivity — the sense of an individual alone, outside society with no firm sense of his or her own place in a rationally ordered scheme.'[7] By subjectivity he does not mean here the experience and consciousness of individuals, but loneliness and isolation. He says that 'Personal life was characterised by its subjectivity — the search for a personal identity outside the social division of labour.'[8] Here again subjectivity connotes social isolation. Later he uses the word in a slightly different sense, this time to mean self-centredness: in the bourgeois ideology 'personal life is an entirely subjective phenomenon having meaning only for the individual.'[9] Elsewhere he uses the word in yet another sense, to mean merely 'personal': he speaks of 'the emphasis on subjective or personal life that distinguishes the petty-bourgeois tradition.'[10] So Zaretsky uses the word 'subjective' to mean three different things: 'isolated', 'self-centred' and 'personal'.

Since he uses the word so inconsistently it is hard to know what meaning to attach to his statement that, with the rise of capitalism, personal life became increasingly subjective. He could mean that it became more isolated, more self-centred, or more personal. In fact, I think he means all three. He means that, with the dissolution of communal ties and the intrusion of exchange relations into every corner of our lives we have become more isolated from one another. He means that, with the emergence of a philosophy and ethos of competition, people have become more self-centred. And he means that personal relations (an expression which he sometimes uses interchangeably with 'subjective relations') emerged out of social relations, whereas before the split between home and work they did not have a distinct existence. The first two hypotheses are quite reasonable, and there is no reason to disagree with them. Modern life has undoubtedly meant more isolation both for individuals and for families, and people *do* seem to be increasingly self-centred and concerned with their subjective experiences. But the third hypothesis is quite wrong. There have been personal relations as long as there have been people, and they have always been distinguished by their subjectivity. They did not 'rise' with the rise of capitalism, and they will not fall with its fall.

I cannot help feeling that there is more than confusion behind this third hypothesis. Throughout his book Zaretsky uses the word 'subjective' in a carping way. He seems to prefer the objective yet abstract material of social relations, which is amenable to theory and analysis, to the subjective yet concrete texture of the personal, which is always so cussedly particular. The result of his preference is that he obscures the importance of experience and consciousness in personal life. It becomes increasingly plain that *Capitalism, the Family and Personal Life* is a subtle attack on personal life.

Zaretsky denies that personal life is autonomous or that we can understand it by explaining it in its own terms. It has, he says, to be understood in terms of social relations. Although he comments briefly on the usefulness of psychoanalysis he has more to say against it than in favour of it, arguing that it cannot illuminate the relationships within a family. Psychology in general, according to Zaretsky, does not help us to understand personal life, but distorts our perception of it. He believes that personal life is governed by the laws that govern society as a whole, and that it should be explained by means of a unified social theory, which comes readily to hand in the form of marxism. He does not want to confine marxism to the study of social relations, or to combine it with psychoanalysis in the way that Reich did. He would use marxism to explain the emotions, sexuality, infancy, childhood, the instincts, ageing, sickness and death.

This is a pretty grandiose scheme. Zaretsky does not seem particularly discomfited by the fact that medical science has discovered a considerable amount about ageing, sickness and death without the help of marxism, and he does not hesitate before dismissing psychology with the sweep of an arm, nor does he pause before claiming that marxism, which is a method designed for the study of society, can be applied to personal relations. Marx would not have made such a claim. Before lapsing into positivism Marx indicated that personal relations were outside society. Society, he said, does not consist of individuals, it consists of the social relations in which individuals find themselves.[11] He intended to discover the laws of society, not the laws of personal relations, psychology or medicine. The application of marxism to every sphere of human knowledge was precisely what marked its degeneration under Stalin.

In arguing that personal life, subjectivity, psychology and physiology should be explained in social terms, Zaretsky reveals a similar mistake to economism. He does not exactly reduce personal life to an outgrowth of the means of production, but he does try and explain it in terms of economic life, with the result that personal life evaporates into social abstractions.

It is sad that a book that looked so promising should turn out to be so disappointing. Zaretsky is one of the few people to have grasped the issues that personal politics raises. He realises that the relation of personal life to politics and society is very important and that there is much confusion about it. He also realises that traditional marxism cannot solve this problem. But in the end he does not really make any clearer the relation of politics to personal life, and he is far too reluctant to let go of marxism. The historical material in his book is interesting, but it does not make things any clearer, for no amount of historical evidence will help if you cannot perceive the essential difference between personal life and social life. If you ignore subjective experience and individuality, and try to put in its place objective facts and social abstractions, you will lose sight of the personal entirely. That is what happens to Zaretsky.

9. Personal Life in History

According to Zaretsky personal life and the interest in subjective experience are products of history and peculiar to the age we live in. They are not an essential part of human life, but are associated with a particular mode of production. Zaretsky does not state the matter as baldly as this, but that is what his argument amounts to. Events in the past gave rise to subjectivity and personal life, and changes in the future (the not-too-distant future, Zaretsky hopes) will force their decline.

The events to which Zaretsky refers are these. Capitalism organised production in such a way that men were taken out of the home for a large part of the day and women were confined to it. Thus the personal became detached from men's work and became attached to women's work. The personal and the social separated. Conditions in capitalist factories were much worse than those in both the artisan's workshop and the peasant's smallholding. Wage labour alienated people from their work, bad conditions drove men to seek solace in the bosom of their families, and the separation between the personal and the social was thereby made worse.

The relationship between home and work, men's roles and women's roles, the social and the personal *have* altered in much the way he describes. As an account of historical trends the book has much to recommend it, but Zaretsky overstates the case against personal life, and he is wrong in the details. Home and work have, it is true, become separated from one another over the centuries — but the home was a predominantly female sphere and public life a predominantly male sphere long before capitalism. We find in the middle ages, for example, women of all classes confined to the home and excluded from both secular and ecclesiastical adminstration. Conditions of work during the industrial revolution were, it is true, very cruel — but feudal peasants, bound in serfdom to their lords, also worked long and hard for the benefit of someone else, and also had their surplus produce expropriated. We have to ask whether *modern* conditions of work are so much worse that they make workers seek all their happiness at home. Home life today is, it is true, more important than it was — but peasants in medieval Europe had such poor homes that the sort of home life we enjoy today was not possible then. For life to centre on the home there has to be a home where people can spend their time in comfort, and there has to be some prospect of decent recreation within it. Increased leisure and higher standards of living have probably been more responsible for home-centred activities than bad conditions of work.

It is not history that forces us to say that personal relations existed in pre-capitalist society; it is commonsense. As long as there have been people there have been face-to-face relations between them, and no theory, however sophisticated, can get over that. There is, however, evidence that people thought about and valued their personal relations in pre-capitalist society.

Rather than trying to cover a long historical period like Zaretsky does I want to confine my attention to the late middle ages. This was a period of transition. Feudal society, whose decay had begun in the twelfth century, underwent shocks and tremors in the fourteenth century that brought an old way of life swiftly to an end. During the fourteenth century there existed feudal lords and merchant capitalists, bound serfs and free peasants, labourers and master craftsmen. Even when we consider a single century it is possible to oversimplify, and we should bear in mind that in some parts of Europe feudalism had vanished earlier, while in others it was to persist into the nineteenth century. Nevertheless, we can see in the fourteenth century a feudal way of life which capitalism was rapidly eroding.

Men's work and women's work

In feudal Europe, peasant women as well as peasant men worked outside the home. Women were required to do unpaid labour for the lord of the manor, and they were known to do rough field work and rough building work alongside men. They took their place, for example, among the labourers on the building sites of Chartres, Canterbury, and Strasbourg. But, like modern working women, they usually did different work from men. A decree of Charlemagne, issued in 827, listed the customary work of men and women. Men's work included ploughing, tending the vine, reaping, moving, hedging, fencing, quarrying and building, while women's work included textile work, woolcarding, making clothes, washing clothes and shearing sheep.[1] So rigid was the sexual division of labour in France at this time that women were put in separate compounds to do their work. William Langland, in *Piers the Ploughman*, reflects a fourteenth-century conception of women's work that is not very different from the modern one.[2] In Montaillou, a Pyrennean village, we discover a comparable division of labour. Men ploughed, harvested, hunted and fished. 'Women were in charge of water, fire, the garden, cooking and gathering kindling.'[3] The sexual division of labour between women and men corresponded more or less to the division between indoors and outdoors.[4]

Among the merchant class at this time trade was a sphere from which most women were excluded. There were some women traders in the middle ages, and in York the widows of guildsmen were permitted to carry on the family business, and it has been said that 'the women traders of medieval London were persons of strong character, an undeniable business ability, and that they played a not inconsiderable part in the industrial life of the city.'[5] However the craft guilds usually excluded women, and career women of the fourteenth century were not typical.

Among the bourgeoisie of the fourteenth century women were confined to their homes as much as modern housewives are. Their husbands, by contrast, were actively involved not only in economic activities but in public life as well. Public affairs were a predominantly upper-class preserve, though other classes engaged in them to a lesser degree. Successful merchants frequently went away on business trips. Powerful aristocrats were engaged in politics as well as the management of their estates. On the estate itself there were offices reserved to men of the lower classes — for example, on English estates the steward and bailiff were called away from home from time to time to inspect one manor or another. Other men in the English village also had duties outside the home, attending the hundred or shire moot, or serving as sidesmen to an archidiaconal or ruridecanal visitation.[6] Women were excluded from all these activities, and in England were also excluded from some of the legal duties imposed on men. When the lord of the manor took legal action to recover a runaway serf he had to produce two of the absconder's kinsfolk as witnesses but women were debarred from witnessing.[7] The church reserved all public activities and positions of authority to men, except for authority within female monastic orders. No priest, canon, deacon or bishop was ever a woman.

Poor women were not so confined to the home, not because the household was a unit of production, but because the poor had no home worth speaking of. It is difficult to imagine the poverty of some medieval peasants. The poorest lived in tiny, two-roomed cottages with mud walls and a thatched roof. Their construction was so flimsy that they could be taken down and carried away. There was no chimney, the smoke finding its way through the door. There was little furniture and few household goods — a few pots and bowls, some forks and spoons, some stools and a trestle table. Beds were almost unknown, and the peasant slept on a straw-filled mattress cast upon the floor.

Because of the limited social wealth even middle-class homes were poor by modern standards. Chimneys were not widespread until the sixteenth century, and glass was rare. One of the wealthiest homes in late thirteenth-century Colchester contained only the following possessions: a trestle table (and doubtless some settles and stools, though the inventory does not mention them) two silver spoons, a cup, a table cloth and two towels, a brass cauldron, a brass dish, a washing basin and ewer, a trivet and iron candlesticks, two beds (indicative of the owner's wealth) two gowns, a mantle, one piece of russet cloth, 3lb wool, two barrels and a butcher's stock in trade.[8] This inventory is probably incomplete, as it was drawn up by the butcher for tax purposes, but it gives an idea of the spartan conditions of the period. Even as late as the seventeenth century the domestic interiors of the bourgeoisie — as portrayed by artists like de Hooch and Vermeer — were remarkably frugal by modern standards.

In the peasant hovel housework as we know it was impossible. Since poor peasants could not be houseproud in the modern sense, women could not be completely identified with the home. The closer identification of women with the home has come about because of higher standards of living. Now that the home is an important centre of consumption the job of home-maker is possible and women's ancient identification with home and family takes on a new significance.

Servile burdens

How do the working conditions of the medieval peasantry compare with those of the proletariat? The industrial revolution certainly produced conditions far worse than those previously experienced. The textile factory is a case in point. Before the industrial revolution some textile workers had had workshops in their own homes and the whole family had contributed to the work in hand. Although they worked hard, conditions were comparatively good, and it was sometimes possible for a weaver to produce enough in four days to support his family for seven. When weavers moved into the great new mills, the family ceased to work together. The work of each member of the family — women and children included — became gruelling and repetitive, and workers lost the last vestige of control over their own labour. The discipline of the mill took over. A poor peasant in the fourteenth century certainly had advantages over the Lancashire cotton operative of the nineteenth — not least fresh air and the opportunity to produce her own food. Free (as opposed to feudal) peasants worked at an easy pace, unlike proletarians, for whose bosses time is money. The working day of the people of Montaillou, for example, 'was punctuated with long, irregular pauses, during which one would chat with a friend, perhaps at the same time enjoying a glass of wine.'[9] But the bad conditions of industrial work are no proof that a new sphere of personal life emerged.

The conditions of serfs were different from those of free peasants, and contained much to produce alienation. Perhaps this alienation was not equal to that experienced by factory workers, but sufficient to warrant a comparison. The feudal peasant had the right to work a portion of land in return for labour on the lord's demesne or private farm. Three days' work a week on the demesne was normal, and there were calls for extra work in harvest time. Lord's work came first, peasant's work last. Serfs owned nothing at all and were bound from birth to death to the land they occupied; when the land was sold they were sold with it. It is easy for modern city dwellers to romanticise the position of the feudal peasantry, but their work was unbelievably hard, and they knew little rest or recreaction.

Until the introduction of farm machinery agricultural work was, next to mining, the worst that people had to do. Old agricultural labourers still living today can remember the terrible conditions they worked in before the first world war. Even free peasants, with advantages that both serfs and landless labourers lacked, could lead a hard and sorry life. Fourier had a clear idea of the hard life of free peasants. He had little time for romantic notions of peasant life. The sturdy peasants of the literary imagination were, he said, in reality sad and dirty and remarkable for their coarseness. Anyone who had travelled through France and seen the wretched food eaten in the country would hesitate to say the peasant was happier than his counterpart in the city.[10]

Industrial conditions were at their worst during the early decades of the nineteenth century. Since then there has been a gradual improvement, and in the twentieth century they have got much better. Alienation must have been worse in the nineteenth century than the twentieth. Zaretsky says that a new sphere of personal life emerged among the working class in the twentieth century, and he attributes it largely to alienation. However, if personal life emerged among workers in the twentieth century, it could not have been brought about by alienation, and if it was brought about by alienation, it must have emerged before the twentieth century.

In fact, what has emerged in industrial society has been a new type of home life, not a new sphere of life altogether. Changes in home life have come about not because of alienation, nor even because of bad conditions of work. They have come about because of changes in consumption. Industrial production and the exploitation of overseas colonies have increased the living standards of the metropolitan working class, and many more commodities are consumed in the working-class home than there were previously. Improved plumbing, comfortable furniture, a better diet, TV and radio have all made the working-class home a better place to live in than it was a hundred years ago.

A distinct sphere of personal life

Was there a distinct sphere of personal life before capitalism? The *quality* of personal life has changed, but personal life itself was not brought into being by capitalism. In the middle ages people had a personal life and took an interest in it. Perhaps they did not concentrate on it in the same way that we do, or think the individual as important as we do, but it is not true to say that they took no account of their subjective experience and no account of individuals.

A distinct sphere of personal life existed even among the peasantry. Zaretsky denies this because he is incapable of distinguishing the personal from the social. 'Peasants and other pre-capitalist labourers were governed by the same social relations "inside" and "outside" work,' he says; 'the proletarian, by contrast, was a "free" man or woman outside work.'[11] True, the feudal peasant, living and working on the lord's manor, was subject to the lord's authority in every sphere of life; true, people's personal relations are shaped by social forces of which they are often unaware; true, the very poverty of peasant life set definite limits to personal relations; but these things do not mean that there was no personal life among peasants.

Of these personal relations we know little, since little was written about them. The record-keepers of the period found the life of the peasantry uninteresting, and the only personal aspects of peasant life that were of sufficient importance to be written about were those that affected the livelihood of their superiors — for example, a serf's choice of wife. The owner of serfs was as interested in their offspring as in the offspring of his cattle and pigs. In fact, the serf's offspring were often called a 'litter' in English legal documents. The paucity of detail concerning the personal life of the peasantry is such that social historians who want to say something about it are often forced to resort to imagination.

Eileen Power, a great populariser of medieval history, enlivens her account of a peasant's life on the manor of the Abbot of St. Germain des Prés by a considerable amount of informed guesswork, since she can find little concerning him in the Roll of the Abbot. The Roll records his name and that of his wife, the members of his family and the services required of him. His name is Bodo, his wife is Ermentrude, and they have three children; he has a measure of land sufficient to support his family which he holds as a tenant of St. Germain; he has arable, vines and meadow; he pays two silver shillings to the army and two hogsheads of wine for the right to pasture his pigs; every third year he gives timber for fences; he has to plough winter and spring, and every week he gives two labour services and one of handwork; he has to carry when required, and to pay three fowls and fifteen eggs; and he owns half a windmill, for which he pays two shillings.[12] That is all we know about him. The Roll is silent about his personal life. But what does this silence signify? It signifies exactly the same as the silence of a company's annual report on the personal lives of its employees: lack of interest. No-one would conclude from company reports that workers have no personal relations, and no-one should conclude from the silence of manorial rolls that serfs had no personal relations.

The silence is sometimes broken. The roll books record marriages and throw an interesting light on people's struggle to realise their own wishes rather than to be governed by rule and custom. The Inquisitorial register on Montaillou is even more enlightening, and the Inquisition's investigation of the village has left us with an unparalleled record of the personal relations of ordinary people there.

Among the upper classes, dynastic and property considerations were paramount in marriage (though love and personal attraction occurred in sexual relations outside it). Such considerations were unimportant for the peasants, since they had no property. Peasants were usually free to marry whoever they liked, though forced marriages were not unknown.[13] However, when a serf from one manor wished to marry a serf from another, questions of property arose and the lord normally exacted a fine from the peasant marrying out. There were also problems of property when a bond person wished to marry a free person, and in both these cases legal deliberation was required. We have accounts of such deliberations. The right to marry as they pleased was important to serfs, and over the years they established fixed customs: the fine was not to be arbitrary, a serf could buy the right to marry when he came into his father's holding, exemptions from manorial regulation were bargained for, and so on.

It was in the lord's interest to ensure that widows remarried, for they inherited their husband's holdings, but not their duties. Once the lord married off a widow he could have a man in the holding to provide labour services. Not all men who were ordered to marry widows in this way agreed, and those who did not were hauled before the manor court. They were told: 'Either marry, or face a fine. If you cannot pay, your goods will be distrained.' On the Manor of Hales, Thomas Robins of Oldbury appeared before the court on 11 December 1279. He had been ordered to marry Agatha of Halesowen, but had refused, and as there were no guarantors for his fine it was ordered that he should be distrained. In the following six weeks he was brought before the court twice more. On 7 January 1280 he was distrained, and finally, on 23 January, he paid a fine of three shillings rather than enter a marriage he had not chosen. On the same manor, R. Ridyacre found himself in a similar position, but somehow managed to get out of marrying *and* paying the fine.[14]

The peasants' sentiments are rarely recorded in their own words. When they are one gets the sense of shutters being thrown back and a shaft of light striking into a dim interior. Pierre Maury, a Cathar shepherd from Montaillou, felt a conflict between desire and custom which was rather different from that of the men from Hales. He fell in love with a woman of orthodox faith, and there was pressure on him to marry instead a woman whom he shared the Cathar heresy. In about 1302, he went to work for his cousin. 'The following winter I grazed my flock in the Val d'Arques,' he told the Inquisition. 'I lived in the house of my first cousin, Raymond Maulen, of Arques. I fell passionately in love with a girl in the village, Bernadette den Esquinath. And for two years no-one spoke to me of heresy because they could see that I was passionately in love with this girl.' Soon, however, his employer asked him to marry someone more suitable. 'You, Pierre, who used to be so fond of the Cathar goodmen,' said his employer, 'you no longer care about them. And instead you are converted to whoredom. You are looking for a wife. Well, we'll give you one. One who will have good understanding of the [Cathar] faith. And if you have a wife like that, it will be better for you than to have one who does not share our beliefs.'[15] In the end, however, this arranged marriage did not take place, but Pierre stopped seeing Bernadette.

There is clear evidence of a distinct sphere of personal life among other classes as well. Among the upper classes, even though marriage was based on economic calculation, there were individuals who kicked over the traces just as these recalcitrant peasants did. For them too desire and custom sometimes clashed.

Arranged marriages

Arranged marriages were normal in the upper class, and the betrothal often took place when the bride and groom were small children. Whether children or adults, the offspring of landed families were sold to the highest bidder. In the words of G.M. Trevelyan, 'county families regarded the marriages of their children as counters in the game of family aggrandizement, useful to buy money and estates, or to secure the support of powerful patrons.'[16] The fact that marriages were arranged, however, does not mean that people accepted what was arranged, and for some the bonds of these marriages were so onerous that they strained them to bursting. The consequences could be harsh. Elizabeth Paston, the daughter of Norfolk landowners, was destined to marry a widower of fifty. She rebelled at the prospect, and for nearly three months was 'beaten once in the week or twice, sometimes twice in one day, and her head broken [i.e. made to bleed] in two or three places.'[17] Other members of the family managed to get the spouses they wanted without suffering so much. John Paston was allowed to marry Margery Brews, who was not a particularly good match, after persuasion alone, and Margery Paston went so far as to secretly betroth herself to a bailiff on the family estate. She resisted the bullying of her family for many years and was eventually allowed to marry the man of her choice.

Once in a marriage the parties sometimes sought to break out of it. At times the motives were as materialistic as the motives for marriage were in the first place. Charles IV of France, for example, had his marriage to Blanche annulled in the 1320s because she could not provide him with a male heir. A ninth-century bishop complained that men would spend their wives' dowries and then 'shamelessly desert them, delighting in prudent and handsomer and wealthier mates'.[18] But the reason for annulment or divorce was not always mercenary or dynastic: personal dissatisfaction was often cited as a motive. A man would suddenly 'discover' that a marriage contracted on the soundest economic grounds, but not to his liking, was vitiated by some legal impediment — for example, that he and his wife were related within prohibited degrees. Proceedings for annulment would follow. Such proceedings by the nobility were common, and if blood relationship could not be proved, they would try relationship through marriage, and, failing that, some relationship between their godparents. Moralists of the day bewailed the ease with which those who could afford litigation would dissolve their marriages and contract a union with someone more pleasing to them.

These attempts to dissolve arranged marriages show that in the middle ages people did have personal preferences. They were, in a sense, the personal solutions of the age, and they show that personal life as we understand it today existed before capitalism. Evidence about the poor is not as common as evidence about the rich, and litigation to dissolve a marriage was so expensive and time-consuming that it was beyond the reach of the poor. But we have seen that poor men and women were quite capable of exert-ing their personal preferences when attempts were made to force them into a marriage that they found disagreeable.

It is commonly assumed that social convention and personal feeling conflict with one another, and nowhere more so than in love and marriage. It is often argued that love as we experience it today (or romantic love as it is sometimes called) did not exist in pre-capitalist society because marriages were arranged or formed for reasons of convenience; love existed only in the illicit affairs of the rich. I think this argument is mistaken. It is certainly *less* likely that there will be love in a marriage of convenience than in one that is formed with free choice, but it is not out of the question, and there is evidence of love even in marriages that are entered into on solid economic grounds. In Montaillou women made love potions to get their daughters husbands, and the village bailiff spoke gushingly of his love for his wife.[19] A study of Lesquire, a village in Béarn, made in the 1960s, found marriage rules as strict as those in medieval villages, but also found love between couples.[20] I am not saying the feelings these couples have are the same as those of couples who choose to live together for no other reasons than the love they bear for each other, but I am saying that strict social customs do not mean there is no personal life.

10. A City of Strangers

In the long transition from feudal to a capitalist society subjective as well as objective changes undoubtedly occurred in personal life. The question is, however, not whether there have been changes in personal life, but what sort of changes they were. We should not describe them, as Zaretsky does, in terms of the rise of subjectivity or the emergence of personal life. Subjectivity did not 'rise' and personal life did not 'emerge'. What we see in modern society is not a new sphere of personal life, but a new *relation* between the personal and the social.

The separation of work from home and its effect on the family has been one of these changes, but there have been others as well: class relations are maintained more by impersonal mechanisms than they were, wage labour is more important now than personal domination, social relations have got more complex, towns have grown, public life has altered, and intimacy in personal relations has become highly esteemed. If we had to sum up these changes we would have to say they amount to the rise of social life and the devitalisation of public life. In this chapter I want to say how they came about.

Personal domination

In feudal society, lords and peasants lived close to each other. Lords who did not spend the whole time on an estate (they often had more than one), delegated authority to bailiff, reeve, hayward and beadle. The number of office-holders was small, and the class structure was both simple and visible. All these things made class relations very personal. Although social relations in the countryside have changed a lot, there are still more personal relations between members of different classes in the country than there are in the cities: farmworkers still know the man in 'the big house'.

Power in feudal society was based on the ownership of land.

The lord of a manor would often hold his land on tenure from a greater lord, and, as his serfs submitted to him, so he would submit to his overlord. An overlord might in turn owe fealty to an even greater lord. A landowner's power reached as far as those immediately below him, but no further. The king of England, for example, had direct power over the great dukes and barons, but not over those who were subjects of the dukes and barons. A land holder gave his landlord personal services rather than rent. Kings demanded military service from the great landowners, and great landowners demanded that lesser landowners raise men when the call for military service came. At the bottom of the pyramid the serf gave her own labour to the lord as and when it was required.

In European feudal society there were few bureaucracies — certainly none so complex as those of today, when we have the impression of dealing with a completely impersonal organisation. Everyone in it seems faceless, no-one is personally responsible for anything, and nothing ever seems to happen, though one moves from room to room and waits an eternity in corridors. The complexity of bureaucratic organisations, their endless rules and regulations, their rigid division of labour, and the fact that any authority in them attaches to the office rather than the person, all combine to create this impersonal power. In feudal society, however, power attached to the person rather than the office. In the adminstration of justice, for example, there was little uniformity. Peasants might be subject to the caprice of the local landowner, and they struggled continually for customary rights.

It was not only in adminstration that the social and the personal mingled, but in the economy as well. Production was simple, and trading was not extensive. The material interdependence of millions, such as we have today, did not exist. Nearly all that the land produced was consumed by those who lived on it or nearby. The economy was overwhelmingly agricultural and there were few townspeople to feed. The life of the majority was simple and was little affected by trade. With the passage of centuries trade became more extensive and people were brought into indirect contact with an ever widening circle of people. The labourer Adam Smith described had precious little personal contact with anyone who contributed to the production of his garment. The medieval peasant, by contrast, could identify many of those whose labour went into the manufacture of his coat — the shepherd, the weaver and the tailor, all of whom may have lived in the same village.

Capitalism grew out of trade, and as markets increased demand the production of goods for consumption turned into the production of commodities for exchange. Exchange came to dominate all relations of production, and everything came to have a cash value. As feudal relations withered, personal services were replaced by money rents and wage labour. In wage labour the personal character of social relations vanishes completely and is transformed into yet another relation of exchange.

In feudal society the idea of personal life was weak not because there were no distinct personal relations, but because there were few distinct social relations. Only when people came to be dominated by the impersonal relations of the market was personal life thrown into sharp contrast. The social receded into obscurity and the personal became brightly illuminated.

The growth of towns

In medieval England, nine out of ten people lived in small villages. Medieval townsfolk, originally bound by the same feudal relations as villagers, gradually bought their freedom from lord or king, bishop or abbot, and the towns were granted charters of self government. Towns were small and close-knit, and life in them was not very different from that in the country. The relation between a master and his apprentices or journeymen remained as personal as that between serf and lord, and most people knew one another by sight. Only with the growth of the urban population in the seventeenth century did there emerge a city where life in public was a perpetual encounter with strangers.

Between 1350 and 1750 the population of England grew slowly, then there was a rapid increase. Partly as a result of this growth in population and partly as a result of the enclosure of agricultural land, the countryside contained a surplus of people. Many migrated to the towns, where new trades and occupations were crying out for new workers.

London expanded rapidly in the seventeenth century, and it has been estimated that between 1650 and 1750 there was an annual influx of 8,000 new residents, making it the largest city in Europe.[1] This urban immigration was qualitatively different from the urban immigration of the late middle ages. Those who had gone to the towns in the fourteenth century had carried the stigma of serfdom and had been subject to numerous restrictions. In the seventeenth and eighteenth centuries, however, there was a great demand for wage labour, and this made a welcome for all hands.

This rapid migration disturbed the social order. Firstly, the expansion of trade created many new occupations, and in a society where occupations were highly organised, each with a definite status, it was difficult to accommodate new ones socially. There were, for example, many new clerical and office jobs. Previously, people in different occupations had worn different types of clothing, which made it easy to identify those one met in public and easy to assign them to their proper position in society. Now it was not so easy. Secondly, people were placed socially by their family as much as by their occupation, but the people who migrated from the countryside were often single, and therefore of unknown origin. Defoe described those who came to the city as a 'motley mass'.[2]

Strangers living close to one another, and routinely encountering one another in public, are common enough today, and we take it for granted that we should know nothing about those we meet in public. A person's appearance tells us nothing apart from the sharpest differences of class and culture, and strangers need to tell us quite a lot about themselves before we can place them. In the late seventeenth and early eighteenth century it was new and somewhat disturbing to find oneself cheek-by-jowl with others of uncertain rank and antecedents.

By 1700 the metropolis had become a place where it was often hard to assess those one met, but the constant rubbing of shoulders with strangers had a positive result. It created a vital public life and a type of sociability that we find hard to comprehend. Because the hierarchies were disturbed and public encounters were uncertain, there developed personal relations in public that were formal and lacking in intimacy, yet still friendly and convivial. This vital public life was limited because, although it permitted a considerable intermingling of classes, it was exclusively masculine. It was also to be temporary. The renewed expansion of great centres like London in the nineteenth century was to drive personal relations out of the public sphere.

The manners of the upper class in the seventeenth century had permitted relative strangers to engage in personal comment of a kind that we would today describe as intimate. The court, which dominated upper-class life in western Europe, was extremely formal, but those who met there had prior personal knowledge of one another, since it was quite small. Consequently people engaged in florid and formal greetings that referred to the qualities and achievements of those they addressed. There was gossip and tittle-tattle about everyone's doings and failings, and in conversation between people of unequal status the one of higher rank was free to interrogate the other concerning the most personal rumours that might be circulating.[3] This social world, in which artificiality and malice were common, was satirised by Molière in *Le Misanthrope*, whose hero Alceste had such a sincere contempt for these manners that he was dismissed as a fool by those around him. Molière presented *Le Misanthrope* at the *Palais Royal* in 1666, where, not surprisingly, it received a cool welcome.

In the eighteenth century the court's pre-eminence waned. Its decline, and the incursion of unidentifiable strangers into the metropolis, contributed to the exclusion of personal comment from polite conversation. In 1750 Lord Chesterfield cautioned his son to avoid self-disclosure and personal allusions when he made new friends. Voltaire warned against gossip, and the compliments he employed in his correspondence were indifferent to the character of those he addressed. In Marivaux's *La Vie de Marianne* (1741), the heroine notes at her first Parisian dinner party that the conversation is easy yet lacking any reference to those she may not herself have heard of. She is encouraged to talk freely, yet not compelled to disclose any personal information.

Our modern belief that personal relations are impossible without intimacy makes us doubt whether the rituals of the seventeenth century or the scrupulous avoidance of personal comment in the eighteenth could have been conducive to genuine personal relations. The life of the time, however, ought to make us ponder over the relationship between intimacy and sociability.

The large cities of the late seventeenth and early eighteenth century provided unparalleled opportunities for meeting people and for relaxed, unhurried conversation of a non-intimate kind. There was a variety of institutions where men could gather together and talk: taverns, ale houses, mug houses, social clubs and coffee houses. The most important of these were the coffee houses.

The coffee houses

The first coffee house was opened in Oxford in 1650, the first in London two years later. By 1708 Hatton claimed in his *New View of London* that there were 'near three thousand' in the capital.[4] In a coffee house a man could eat, drink coffee, and sometimes chocolate (but no intoxicating beverage) and talk or receive news. Anyone who could pay a penny was free to enter, and no man was excluded who kept the rules of the house. It was not uncommon for a man to spend two hours in the morning and another two hours in the afternoon in a coffee house, and many people conducted their business there. 'By spending three pence in a coffee house,' said Samuel Johnson, 'he might be for some hours every day in very good company; he might dine for six-pence, breakfast on bread and milk for a penny, and do without supper.'[5] These prices put coffee houses within the reach of some working men,[6] though their normal clientèle ranged from gentry and professions to tradesmen and artisans. Courtiers seldom attended, nor did very poor working men. The equality among those who did attend was recorded in the rough verse of a coffee house broadside:

> First, Gentry, Tradesmen, all are welcome hither,
> And may without Affront sit down Together:
> Pre-eminence of Place, none here should Mind,
> But take the next fit seat that he can find:
> Nor need any, if Finer Persons come,
> Rise up for to assigne them to his Room.[7]

Within the coffee house gradations of rank were overlooked, and it was considered bad manners to touch on a person's social origin.

Conversation and story-telling were highly valued, and being a stranger to the assembled company was not a bar to joining in. One entered, paid one's penny at the counter and took one's place at one of the long tables at which everyone sat. A wide range of popular and intellectual topics was discussed, and in one coffee house a visitor heard men talking about theology, Euclid, the theatre, balls, masques and taxation. The atmosphere of the coffee house seems to have been robust, lively and free.

The coffee houses declined for several reasons in the second half of the eighteenth century, the most important being the rise of the club. Thousands of clubs opened in the late eighteenth century, some of them started by coffee house cliques. Many were more working class than the coffee houses — street clubs and tavern clubs, for example. Some were, or became, more upper-class — such as the gentlemen's clubs of St. James's. With the rise of the club and the decline of the coffee house, the chances of striking up an acquaintance with anyone one met diminished. A great centre of sociability passed away. Coffee houses turned into taverns or chop houses, or closed down completely.

Nothing quite like the coffee house exists today. In Britain the nearest thing is the pub, and pubs with a local clientèle can be extremely convivial, but pubs do not have the long tables which everyone in a coffee house was expected to share, and it is certainly not expected that a stranger will join the assembled company and take part in their conversation. In France people can spend a large part of the day in pavement cafes, but, as in the pub, relations between strangers are restricted. In Germany men join informal drinking circles which meet in a bar the same night every week, and address men they meet nowhere else by the familiar *du*, but these circles are clubs rather than open gatherings. In southern European countries men gather in bars and cafes, but they thrive best in villages and small towns where the men are already acquainted.

The devitalisation of public life

Even as London responded to the influx of the seventeenth century, changes were taking place in the urban environment which were to have an effect on public life. The garden squares of London were conceived not so much as concourses where strangers could gather and talk, but as spaces which one looked at or walked across. Bustle and activity was to be avoided, and deliberate attempts were made to eliminate stalls, acrobats, traders, and pavement cafes.[8] In the latter part of the eighteenth century the new parks encouraged walking rather than lingering in a way the crowded streets and open squares of earlier days had not. In their promenades through the park people made encounters more selectively than they had done in coffee houses, and in the park there emerged the idea of silence in public. In the modern northern European city silence has become the first rule of correct behaviour. Talking indiscriminately to strangers is considered to be a sign of drunkenness or insanity. This rule of silence has helped to confine personal relations to the private sphere, and personal contact between strangers today is perfunctory, hesitant and apologetic.

In the nineteenth century London's population rose from 860,000 to five million. At the centre of the city the working class were crowded into insanitary tenements where families had to make do with the tiniest of spaces and between which courts and alleys filled with a teeming humanity. London in the nineteenth century was overgrown and overcrowded, and in it people had become isolated and afraid. Engels described it in the following terms:

> The very turmoil of the streets has something repulsive, something against which human nature rebels. The hundreds of thousands of all classes and ranks crowding past each other, are they not all human beings with the same qualities and powers, and with the same interest in being happy? And have they not, in the end, to seek happiness in the same way, by the same means? And still they crowd by one another as though they had nothing in common, nothing to do with one another, and their only agreement is the tacit one, that each keep to his own side of the pavement, so as not to delay the opposing streams of the crowd, while it occurs to no man to honour another with so much as a glance.[9]

Towards the end of the century, with public-health legislation, stricter building standards, and the first municipal dwellings, there was some improvement in working-class housing conditions. These changes created conditions that intensified private life and continued to weaken public life. Gross overcrowding had led working-class families to become jealous of their privacy and to desire their own front door. The emergence of com-

munities in the midst of the urban maelstrom created a social life
centred on a few streets where one could meet friends and
relations, and where strangers and outsiders could be easily identified. The city became a collection of villages.

In the twentieth century the sense of disgust which Engels
felt has become even more intense. For the Situationist Raoul
Vaneigem urban life is a metaphor for alienation, and he describes
in poetic terms the isolation he feels in the great city:

> A man carried along by a crowd, which only he can see,
> suddenly screams out in an attempt to break the spell, to
> call himself back to himself, to get back inside his own
> skin. The tacit acknowledgements, fixed smiles, lifeless
> words, listlessness and humiliation sprinkled in his
> path suddenly surge into him, driving him out of his
> desires and his dreams and exploding the illusion of be-
> ing together. People touch without meeting; isolation
> accumulates but is never realised; emptiness overcomes
> us as the density of the crowd grows.[10]

For Vaneigem city life is a 'sterilised zone of impersonal relationships', and he regards it with disgust. He prefers passionate relationships, and he is reluctant 'to stop a stranger to ask him the
way or to "pass the time of day".'[11] He insists on choosing between intimacy and silence. This revulsion against city life, and
against insincere communication in particular, expresses a revulsion against public life itself, and a preference for the intimate
relationships that only private life affords.

Social life has become complex and has separated itself
from personal relations. The city has carried all before it. At
first the great commercial centres responded to the 'motley
mass' with a lively and convivial public life. Later, as urban conditions got worse public life declined. Personal relations became
identified with intimacy, and were thereby privatised.

The idea of fusing the personal and the political expresses a
wish to break down the barriers between the private and public,
between intimate and non-intimate relations. But breaking down
the barriers will not improve public life, and the idea that we
should is part of the process that led to the devitalisation of
public life. The idea of fusing the personal and the political is, in
fact, a product of the city of strangers. It is a part of the
problem, not the solution.

11. Revitalising Public Life

When John Lennon's death was announced on the radio, hundreds of New Yorkers made their way to his home and stood together in the street outside. Some stood quietly, others played his songs on cassette recorders. Spontaneously a large number of people responded to the news by leaving their homes and going to a public place. It was not just a pilgrimage to a pop hero's apartment block. They were compelled by a need to be with others who were strangers to them. 'I couldn't bear to sit alone,' said one young man. 'I had to get out into the street where I could be with other people.' A public figure, who was seen by many as the symbol of a generation, had to be mourned in public.

Crowds and cities

Public life has become frightening. 'Street wise' expresses the modern fear of public life: you have to be shrewd and on the defensive. But public life has not vanished altogether, and it is doubtful whether it ever could. In street-wise cities it exists in a weak and retreating form, taking tragedy, anger or jubilation to bring it to life. The tragedy of John Lennon's death drew out a respectful vigil, followed several days later by larger vigils in Central Park and Liverpool. The deaths of national leaders are mourned in formal parades that draw huge crowds. Tito's death in Yugoslavia and Churchill's death in Britain were both events of this kind — more than mere spectacles, for people wept in the street.

Personal anger and political discontent also bring people into the street. Peaceful demonstrations and violent riots alike create emotions, more or less intense, that one cannot feel in private. Celebrations at the end of war turn private joy into public elation. As news of the armistice spread through Britain in 1918, people stopped work and surged into public places.

November 11 became a carnival day as buses were commandeered by revellers in fancy dress and parties were held in the street. These celebrations lasted three days, getting wilder and wilder until they were finally stopped by the police. There were similar scenes on VE day in 1945. Not all peace celebrations are good-humoured however. When the peace treaty was signed in 1919, an official parade held by the Luton town council was swamped by discharged servicemen angrily demanding work. The mayor and other officials were chased into the town hall by a large crowd, and were besieged there for eight hours while celebrations and rioting took place. Finally the town hall was burned down, the councillors narrowly escaping, while a crowd of thousands sang 'Keep the Home Fires Burning' to the accompaniment of looted pianos.[1] The presence of large numbers has an effect on people that relations in private do not have. Hindus believe that the feeling that comes from being in a devotional crowd is religious, and gatherings of many people, sometimes hundreds of thousands, is one of India's cultural traditions.

Audiences do not have the same effect on their participants that celebrations, riots and religious gatherings do. Often audiences have very little effect on their members at all. They have often been criticised because they are passive gatherings. There is supposed to be something bad about passivity, and it is thought that people should participate rather than watch. When people complain about the passivity of audiences they overlook their importance as an opportunity for people to come together. (I am not sure whether the point about passivity is true anyway: watching *is* an activity.) A society which does not provide people with the opportunity for spectacle is one in which public life has shrunk away to nothing. What we should regret is not the passivity of audiences but the fact that the really big audiences of the past have gone. The vast cinema audiences of the thirties have dwindled under the impact of television. The picture palaces with their big foyers and exotic decor have either closed or been divided up into tiny and rather ordinary-looking cinemas. Political meetings in the open air and in public halls have been superceded by party political broadcasts. Most political meetings now are gatherings of the faithful.

Public communication is gradually being replaced by mass communication. Probably a larger number of people watch a popular television programme than ever watched a cinema film, but the sense of event has been lost. Certainly more people hear a politician give a party broadcast than ever went to a single meeting, but the politician is not a public speaker any more. Instead of a crowd he addresses a family with a TV dinner. With the introduction of radio in the 1920s, political meetings ceased to be important events, and politicians learned a new style of speech. Orators who had hitherto been used to speaking in the open air had to learn to speak in a manner appropriate to the broadcasting studio. Speakers of the old school, like Lloyd George and Ramsay Macdonald, could not adapt. The pipe-sucking Stanley Baldwin, with his homely note and his fireside chats, adapted well. Harold Wilson struck a similar note in the 1960s, and was the first British politician to deal successfully with the TV cameras. Major political organisations now have no need of public meetings. Only small groups, denied access to the mass media, have to use them.

Public space is not enough to create public life. There is public space in cities, but much of it is dead. Large tracts separate tower blocks, but they are wildernesses without life. Squares in town centres are sometimes like wildernesses even though they are filled with people. Leicester Square, at the heart of London's entertainment land, is usually full up, especially on summer evenings: it has been closed to traffic and landscaped; and yet everyone there is either passing through or hanging about aimlessly. An unusual event in the square will create an audience and bring people together for a moment. Not long ago, a street theatre group, the Demolition Decorators, gave unauthorised performances and brought Leicester Square to life. With great difficulty, the police forced their way through the dense crowd and arrested them.

A common life needs order. The problem of the city is that it lacks order of the right kind: about the only order that administrators care about is crime prevention and the free flow of traffic, but the order we need is one that allows us to communicate with others while at the same time defending our personal space. The cult of intimacy and the disorder of cities make it difficult for us to strike this balance. We are together, but we remain silent and avoid each other's gaze. This is partly due to the growth of cities, but there is something other than size and scale that causes it. As Hannah Arendt puts it, the problem of mass society is not that there are so many people in it, but that 'the world between them has lost its power to gather them together, to relate and separate them'.[2] She says that life in mass society is like a spiritualistic séance in which people gathered round a table see it suddenly vanish from their midst; they sit opposite one another, they are no longer separated, but nothing holds them together any more. Personal relations in public have become like this. We squeeze together in a crowded bus, bottom lightly touching bottom, nothing separates us, but nothing holds us together. Greater intimacy is not the answer. It can bring people together as they need to be in private, but it cannot separate them as they need to be in public. Intimacy in public removes the table at the séance. It erodes formality and order, and calls for sincerity which is out of place.

Cities are more than mere collections of buildings, each used for a particular purpose and linked by streets whose only function is to join them up. The city should be something that creates space in which people can come together, and buildings should be things that enhance that space with their beauty and the human achievement they embody. Public life is not just something that exists in the present; it stretches back in time and reaches forward to the future. As something we all share, it embraces our common history and aspirations. The towns of the past — sixteenth-century Rome, seventeenth-century Versailles, eighteenth-century Edinburgh and nineteenth-century Munich — created this public life for a small section of society. Modern cities generally fail to do even that, and although there is no point in hankering after the small ordered cities of the past, any more than there is in trying to recreate the coffee houses of the 1700s, still it is useful to understand the changes that have taken place and that need to be made now. We cannot reconstruct the classic city, nor would we want to, because it reflected the class divisions of its age; but we can change the way in which cities are planned, built and used.

If cities are to become places where there is a vital, democratic public life, changes other than planning and architectural changes are needed. A precondition for it is that men stop dominating public life. I am not talking about men's appropriation of public office (though that must stop as well) but about men's control of public places. Men control public space like colonisers a conquered territory, and women live in public like a subject people. Women have been excluded from public places for a long time. Their exclusion from public office until comparatively recently has stopped them travelling much and has kept them in their homes and local communities. They have also been kept out of public gatherings. The convivial life of the coffee house was for men only, and many clubs were too. There are still clubs and bars closed to women. Chaperoning imposed restrictions on upper-class and middle-class women that men of their class were free from. Chaperoning was also partly designed to protect women from men in public places. Today, unchaperoned women have to put up with repeated harrassment in the streets, and this makes many women have different feelings about public life from men.

The need for boundaries

Traditional politics is not much concerned with the weakening of public life. The liberal idea of civic duty shows some awareness of public life, but the idea is rather old-fashioned and is not discussed much today. Personal politics is more concerned about it, but in a roundabout way. What we usually hear about in personal politics is not so much how good a vital public life would be, but how bad private life is. The criticism of private life takes several forms, sometimes aimed at individualism, sometimes at subjectivity. Sometimes the criticism is aimed at personal solutions, as in this case: 'Our socialism has to articulate a new vision of human relationships... which helps people recognise the difficulties they face not simply as "individual" and "private", but as public and social.'[3] Other times there is a clear attack on privacy as such.

Georgia Sanger, in the Canadian paper *Open Road*, described an anarchist community whose members had decided to discuss all their personal problems with the whole group. They rejected the idea that personal relations should be a private matter, of concern only to the individuals in them, and practised what they called 'the deprivatisation of personal life'. Sanger believes that socialism entails the abolition of privacy.

> People are beginning to recognise that a commitment to the destruction of private property... implies a commitment to radical alternatives... The alternatives include communal living environments and deprivatised personal lives. In fact, a lot of us treat our private lives

as though they were the last vestige of private property.[4]

This idea has some currency in personal politics. It was also expressed in *Solidarity*, a British libertarian socialist magazine, by 'Luciente'. She noted that attitudes to the family have become liberalised in recent years, and that even quite respectable people now question lifelong monogamy. Trendy magazines and even church leaders now say that sex outside marriage is permissible. But the purpose of this liberalisation is to save failing marriages, and attitudes to the couple remain basically unchanged. 'The couple relationship is totally a private one and exclusive of all others.'[5] She comes to the same conclusion as Sanger: 'We aim at abolishing *all* private property relationships... In this desire the family can be no exception.' Nor can the couple. For Sanger and 'Luciente' the argument goes roughly as follows: socialism gets rid of everything to do with capitalism; capitalism is based on private property; therefore socialism should get rid of everything private, which means abolishing privacy.

This argument is remarkably tenacious. Marx had to deal with it a hundred and forty years ago when it was put forward by anti-communists who said, in horrified tones, that the communists would abolish all privacy. Under communism, they said, one will not even have the right to the coat on one's back, since it will be held in common like everything else. Marx patiently explained that when communists talked about private property they did not mean things for personal use, but private ownership of the means of production. Production, he said, had become increasingly socialised under capitalism, but the enormous wealth it brought into society was appropriated by a smaller and smaller number of people. Communism will transfer production to the community, but it has no earthly reason for compelling people to share their coats.[6] Marx made the point well enough, but it does not seem to have sunk in, and even socialists began to say that the abolition of capitalism means the abolition of privacy. In the early years of the Russian revolution there were young communards in Moscow who made a principle of sharing their underwear. Now, in the personal politics movement, there are people who advocate much the same thing. In the Moscow communes there was little or no privacy because apartments were hard to come by and large numbers of people had to squeeze into them. Now, however, people talk about the 'deprivatisation of personal life' when their living conditions do not force it on them.

When people talk about abolishing private life they forget the variety of personal relations, from intimate ones between people who know each other well to fleeting ones between strangers, and we have to remember also the range of activities that occur in a normal and balanced life. Some of our activities are appropriate to private places, some of them to public places. It is not always easy to define the boundary between public and private places, but when an action occurs in an inappropriate place we notice it pretty quickly. Homeless people who sleep in public places, such as under the railway bridge at Embankment station in London, suffer poverty not merely in the absence of material goods, but also in the absence of privacy. There is something unnerving in seeing the rows of people bedding down for the night under the railway, not because their beds of milk-crates and cardboard boxes are so inadequate, but because they are doing something private in a public place. They are literally *deprived*. No-one who talks about deprivatising personal life would be prepared to spend a single night like this. Public actions performed in private also make us feel uneasy. I once knew a man who was widely accepted to be the best public speaker in Hyde Park, and I have never in twenty years seen anyone hold an audience the way he could. But he had an irritating habit of talking to people in private as if he were still on a soapbox. The logic of abolishing private life is that one should not object to being addressed as if one were a public meeting, but, again, no-one who talks about deprivatising personal life would put up with this kind of treatment for long.

Erving Goffman has analysed the way that people divide up their world into private and public places, and the way they perform different actions in each. He calls the private places the 'back region' and the public places the 'front region'. One of his examples is taken from a Shetland Isle hotel. In the kitchen, which was the hotel staff's back region, there would be slovenliness, unruliness and rude imitations of distinguished guests. In the front region of dining room and bar the staff were smart, subdued and respectful.[7] Goffman says that front and back regions are not always in fixed places as they were in the hotel, but depend on the groups of people involved and the actions they perform. I think social order and personal sanity depends on our dividing up the world in this way.

A reasonably interesting and satisfying life depends on it as well. Everyone needs the variety that the separation of public from private life offers. To spend one's whole life in private (which for many people means spending their whole life tied to the home) is incomplete and inhuman. Spending one's whole life in public is also incomplete and inhuman, as my community-worker friend discovered after two years of frantic activity, and as politicians and showbusiness people also find.

What I am interested in is the effect on public life of breaking down the boundary between the public and the private. At first sight it may appear that it would have a good effect, and that seems to be the general idea. After all, if privacy is broken down, won't there be a more vital public life as people escape from their little boxes and go out on to the street? This view is quite mistaken. It assumes that public and private life are opposites, forever at war with one another, and that one rises as the other falls. On the contrary, private life and public life are not opposites: they are bound together, and one cannot exist without the other. It is the boundary between them that creates each. Remove the boundary and neither exists any more.

What happens when small groups of people abolish privacy is that intimacy within the group is heightened. Boundaries are broken down within the group, but the boundary between the group and the outside world remains. In fact, it usually becomes stronger because a style of life is created that cuts off members of the group from the outside world far more effectively than the nuclear family does. Public life is not improved at all. Although personal politics talks about public life (saying that people's difficulties are not individual and private, but social and public) it is not really much interested in it. The talk about the social nature of individual difficulties is just a form of social determinism, not an interest in the wider life of streets and cities, audiences and gatherings, strangers together in a public place.

One of the intentions of collectives — living collectives, work collectives or political collectives — is to reduce organisations to a scale that allows everyone to control them. They also overcome the feeling of being lost or irrelevant in a large national organisation. Collectives set up for political purposes have not remained local and isolated, however, and regional and national contacts, federations and co-ordinating bodies have been set up. In *Beyond the Fragments* Hilary Wainwright describes structures the women's movement has set up on the basis of local control and autonomy, and considers the relation between small-group values and the needs of national organisation. *Beyond the Fragments* tried to make the links between socialism and personal politics, and has been eagerly read by many people who want to bring the fragments together without creating a traditional political party. I went to the conference held in Leeds to consider ways of bringing the fragments together and came away with a feeling of disappointment. The conference opened and closed with a plenary session, in which a large hall was packed to the walls, and in between broke up into small discussion groups. This has become an accepted way of organising conferences in the personal politics movement, and some people would like to see all conferences organised this way. I enjoyed the day in Leeds, but felt disappointed because I had travelled two hundred miles, mingled with fifteen hundred people, but spent the day shut up with two little groups. This was a big event, yet the experience was hardly different from the experience one has in the fragments. It was like being in any other little group. There was no sense of a public event, yet that was the experience we should have had.

Public participation

Personal politics has paid a great deal of attention to personal power in social politics, to who speaks and who is silent, who is elevated and who is abased, and it has made a political issue of the way people feel. In doing these things it has quite rightly united the personal and the political. But there is a danger that personal politics might encourage the devitalisation of public life by reducing politics entirely to small collectives. The problems of the modern city can be tackled only by public measures on a large scale. If they are not tackled, people will not get involved in social politics, and will burrow further into their private lives. In certain respects, the collective type of political organisation is *less* attractive to non-joiners than the traditional type because it calls for more commitment and more involvement. Personal politics has had many successes in the women's movement and has involved women who were not interested in politics before. But if it does not come to terms with the boundary between public and private life, and if it does not move towards a form of political involvement not restricted to discussion groups and workshops, personal politics will remain marginal.

One of the most promising political developments in recent years has been the political festival. In continental Europe these are better established than in Britain. The European Communist Parties have been holding them for years, and they are very successful in France and Italy where the Communists have a lot of popular support. The Communist Party of Great Britain has also run annual festivals over the last few years. So have the smaller marxist parties, such as the French Lutte Ouvrière and the British Socialist Workers' Party. The festivals come and go, and attempts have been made to create a more permanent kind of public life in the form of socialist centres. Centres have been opened in Newcastle and London, unaligned with any faction, though leaning very strongly to the far left. Festivals and centres are a good way of creating a friendly form of public activity in which everyone can join, and the principle needs to be taken up and built upon. They do have their shortcomings, though. The centres only attract politically-minded people, so to a lesser extent do the festivals. The very things that make them attractive to some make them unattractive to many more. The important things about revitalising public life is that it must be for everyone, not just those who think in a certain way. The festivals and centres are, in a word, too political. There is still the idea behind them that socialism is only about politics, and that if you have an event that is non-political you are wasting your time. This priggish attitude is what makes the left unappealing to so many people.

I mentioned the armistice and VE celebrations. National celebrations in peacetime can have a similar envigorating effect. The Royal wedding was celebrated in Britain recently with street parties all over the country. Roads were closed to traffic, bunting was hung out, people came out of their houses and into the streets and mixed with one another in a way they do not normally do. The mistake many people on the left made was to see these events purely as expressions of support for the monarchy, rather than the eruption of public conviviality. They missed their importance because they do not generally recognise the importance of public life. The fact that these events were public celebrations is far more important than what their pretext happens to be. It is more important how people *live* than what they *think*. Far too much emphasis is placed on ideology and not enough on living, and until socialists can produce events that fulfill our need for a vital public life people will walk past socialist centres with their drab political debates and straight to street parties.

The scale of modern cities makes the problem of public life hard to solve. Unless we can find ways of planning cities in a new way, events like festivals will have only a marginal effect. Some consideration is being given to planning already. The New Architecture Movement, for example, held a conference in 1979 to discuss how planning and architecture isolate and oppress women in the home. The un-coordinated activities that *Beyond the Fragments* tried to bring together included many in local communities, and several people involved in housing and planning attended the Leeds conference. But many community activities are fighting a rearguard action, preserving old communities from destruction and the people who live in them from the isolation of modern housing estates. If they are not preserving old communities they are trying to create new ones. Local communities stand only on the borderline of public life. The older ones are sometimes bound by ties of kinship, and are highly suspicious of strangers. New ones can form only by gaining a sense of identity against the outside world. Close-knit communities can be parochial in their outlook, unconcerned with wider issues and uninterested in other communities. While local communities remain like this, the planning of cities will continue to be in the hands of planners, architects and developers.

The complexity of the modern economy has meant the rise of social relations which have thrown into contrast the concrete and personal relations of individuals. Politics has become increasingly concerned with the economy, either creating the right social conditions, or planning it directly, and it is therefore understandable that the social and the political should come to be confused. At the same time public life in cities has been damaged so badly that we fear it rather than welcome it. As politics meshes with the economy, and as public life declines, the public dimension of politics is overlooked — as much in personal as in the more traditional kind. The change in the nature of politics that personal politics aims at is really nothing less than a desire to rob it of its public dimension.

Personal politics has become identified with a minority life-style, at times so bizarre that it has little hope of affecting ordinary people. Instead of concerning itself with the way that a *few* people live, it should concern itself with the way that *most* people live, and should turn to the revitalisation of public life. This requires among other things changes both in the results and the method of town planning. We need to have cities that have the vital local communities now being eroded by comprehensive redevelopment and convivial public spaces in which strangers can come together. By a curious irony the architect of the Beaubourg in Paris, which has created a lively public space, is also the architect of a massive office development in London that threatens the existence of a local community. The Beaubourg, however, is used largely by tourists and the Parisian middle class, and the threatened community is largely working-class. This indicates the need for more widespread working-class participation in planning, enabling people to involve themselves in politics more than the periodic election of government allows.

Public life is twofold: it is the life that takes place in public places, and it is the life of social politics. Many people interested in personal politics have paid more attention to community politics than traditional leftists, who concentrate on national and international politics at the expense of local issues. We need even more attention to be paid to community politics. Just as we need to strike a balance between our personal lives and broad social issues, so in community politics we need to strike a balance between parochial and metropolitan concerns. Revitalising public life in this way takes us to the heart of democracy, for real democracy means involving more people in decision making at all levels of society. It also holds out the promise of harmony between the personal and the political, for in public life we can form personal relations that add to those we form in private, while at the same time participating with others in a common world.

Notes

1. The Personal is Political

1. Antonia Raeburn, *The Militant Suffragettes*, London: New English Library 1974, p.183
2. Sara Evans, *Personal Politics*, New York: Knopf 1979, pp.196-199
3. Juliet Mitchell, *Woman's Estate*, Harmondsworth: Penguin 1971, p.85
4. Mitchell, *op.cit.* p.14n. My emphasis.
5. Sue Aspinall, 'Suffocation in a woman's world', *Socialist Challenge*, London: no. 95, 10 May 1979, p.15
6. Chris Knight, *My Sex Life*, London: Women and Labour Collective 1980, p.1
7. Ann Bliss, *Our Sex Lives, Our Strength*, London: Women and Labour Collective 1980, p.6

2. Social Relations and Politics

1. Adam Smith, *The Wealth of Nations*, book 1, chapter 1
2. David McLellan (ed.) *Marx's Grundrisse*, St. Albans: Paladin 1971, p.89
3. Jo Freeman, *The Tyranny of Structurelessness*, Kingston: Anarchist Workers' Association c.1975
4. 'Redstockings Manifesto', in Robin Morgan (ed.) *Sisterhood is Powerful*, New York: Vintage 1970, pp.598-99
5. Bill West, 'Politics, Reich and Feminism', *Energy and Character*, Abbotsbury: vol.10, no.3, September 1979, p.76
6. *Woman's Own*, London: 17 February 1979, pp.22-23
7. Central Office of Information, *Britain 1981*, London: HMSO 1981, p.333
8. Lucy Komisar, *The New Feminism*, London: Watts 1971, p.24
9. *Woman's Own*, ibid.
10. Clara Zetkin, *Conversations with Lenin*, New York: International Publishers 1974, p.49
11. Big Flame, *Towards a Revolutionary Socialist Organisation*, Liverpool: Big Flame 1977, p.3

3. Personal Life

1. G.R. Bach and P. Wyden, *The Intimate Enemy*, London: Souvenir Press 1970, p.1

4. The Politics of Personal Relations

1. Max Farrar, 'Family, capitalism and personal life', *Revolutionary Socialism*, Liverpool: no.1, July 1977, p.28
2. *ibid*.
3. R.D. Laing *The Politics of the Family and Other Essays*, London: Tavistock. 1971, pp. 78-79
4. R.D. Laing, H. Phillipson and A.R. Lee, *Interpersonal Perception*, London: Tavistock 1966, p.83
5. R.D. Laing, *Knots*, Harmondsworth: Penguin 1972, p.19
6. Laing, Phillipson and Lee, *op.cit.* p.15
7. Eric Berne, *Games People Play*, London: André Deutsch 1966, p.84
8. Nancy M. Henley, *Body Politics*, Englewood Chiffs: Prentice Hall 1977, p.3
9. *ibid*. pp.101-108
10. Matthew Israel, 'Irritations and jealousies', in Rosabeth Kanter (ed.) *Communes*, New York: Harper & Row 1973, pp.397-399

5. The Cult of Intimacy

1. G.R. Bach and P. Wyden, *The Intimate Enemy*, London: Souvenir Press 1970, pp.30-31
2. Richard Sennett, *The Fall of Public Man*, Cambridge: Cambridge University Press 1977, p.5
3. Red Therapy Group, *Red Therapy*, London: Red Therapy c.1975, p.23
4. Jo Freeman, *The Tyranny of Structurelessness*, Kingston: Anarchist Workers' Association, c.1975, p.3
5. Sheila Rowbotham, Lynne Segal and Hilary Wainwright, *Beyond the Fragments*, London: Merlin Press 1979, p.41

6. Only Connect

1. D.H. Lawrence, *Assorted Articles*, London: Heinemann 1932, pp.151-52
2. *ibid*.
3. Ford Madox Ford, *The Bodley Head Ford Madox Ford*, London: Bodley Head 1971, vol.5, p.445
4. Adam Smith, *The Wealth of Nations*, book 1, chapter 8
5. *The Guardian*, London: 30 April 1979
6. Dory Previn, *The Altruist and the Needy Case*, United Artists' Music 1971

7. B. Bykhovsky, *The Individual and Society*, Moscow: Novosty 1964, p.11
8. K. Marx and F. Engels, *The German Ideology*, in *Karl Marx and Frederick Engels — Collected Works, vol.5*, London: Lawrence and Wishart 1976, p.37
9. *ibid.* p.54
10. David McLellan, *Karl Marx*, St. Albans: Paladin 1977, p.423
11. 'Redstockings Manifesto', in Robin Morgan (ed.) *Sisterhood is Powerful*, New York: Vintage 1979 p.598
12. E.M. Forster, *Howards End*, Harmondsworth: Penguin 1979, p. 195-96

7. Individualism and Personal Autonomy

1. Steven Lukes, *Individualism*, Oxford: Blackwell 1973, p.4
2. *ibid.* p.6
3. *ibid.* p.12
4. Sheila Rowbotham, Lynne Segal and Hilary Wainwright, *Beyond the Fragments*, London: Merlin Press 1979, p.131

8. Capitalism, the Family and Personal Life

1. 'The family, which to begin with is the only social relation, becomes later, when increased needs create new social relations and the increased population new needs, a subordinate one...' K. Marx and F. Engels, *The German Ideology*, in *Karl Marx and Frederick Engels — Collected Works, vol.5*, London: Lawrence & Wishart 1976, p.43
2. Eli Zaretsky, *Capitalism, the Family and Personal Life*, London: Pluto Press 1976, p.29
3. *ibid.* p.39
4. *ibid.* p.57
5. *ibid.* p.82
6. *ibid.* p.18
7. *ibid.* p.30
8. *ibid.* p.34
9. *ibid.* p.82
10. *ibid.* p.63
11. David McLellan (ed.) *Marx's Grundrisse*, St. Albans: Paladin 1971, p.89

9. Personal Life in History

1. Eileen Power, *Medieval People*, Harmondsworth: Penguin 1951, p.24
2. William Langland, *Piers the Ploughman*, Harmondsworth: Penguin 1978, p.81
3. Emmanuel Le Roy Ladurie, *Montaillou*, London: Scolar Press 1979, p.5

4. *ibid.* pp.109-110
5. A. Abram, 'Women traders in medieval London' quoted in C.G. Coulton, *Medieval Panorama*, Cambridge: Cambridge University Press 1939, p.619
6. Coulton, *op.cit.* p.72
7. H.S. Bennett, *Life on the English Manor*, Cambridge: Cambridge University Press 1962, p.310
8. Coulton, *op.cit.* p.310
9. Le Roy Ladurie, *op.cit.* p.278
10. J. Beecher and R. Bienvenu, *The Utopian Vision of Charles Fourier*, London: Jonathan Cape 1972, p.136
11. Eli Zaretsky, *Capitalism, the Family and Personal Life*, London: Pluto Press 1976, p.65
12. Power, *op.cit.* p.183
13. Coulton, *op.cit.* p.78.
14. Bennett, *op.cit.* p.244
15. Le Roy Ladurie, op.cit. pp.78-79
16. Trevelyan, *op.cit.* pp.64-65
17. *ibid.* p.65
18. Coulton, *op.cit.* p.636
19. Le Roy Ladurie, *op.cit.* p.152
20. *ibid.* p.186

10. A City of Strangers

1. E.A. Wrigley, 'A simple model of London's importance in English society and economy, 1650-1950', *Past and Present*: no.37, Oxford 1967, p.46
2. Daniel Defoe, *A Tour Through the Whole Island of Great Britain*, Harmondsworth: Penguin 1971, p.308
3. Richard Sennett, *The Fall of Public Man*, Cambridge: Cambridge University Press 1977, p.61
4. John Ashton, *Social Life in the Reign of Queen Anne*, London: Chatto and Windus 1882, vol.1, p.216
5. James Boswell, *The Life of Samuel Johnson*, Oxford: Oxford University Press 1934, vol.1, p.71
6. In the mid-eighteenth century the weekly wage of a male labourer was about ten shillings, that of a female labourer about seven shillings, and that of skilled craftsman about £3. George Rudé, *Hanoverian London*, London: Secker & Warburg 1971, p.88
7. Aytoun Ellis, *The Penny Universities*, London: Secker & Warburg 1956 pp.46-47
8. Sennett, *op.cit.* p.55
9. Frederick Engels, *The Condition of the Working Class in England*, in *Karl Marx and Frederick Engels — Collected Works vol.4*, London: Lawrence & Wishart 1975, p.329

10. Raoul Vaneigem, *Traite de Savoir-vivre à l'Usage des Jeunes Générations*, part 1, section 3
11. *ibid*. p.37

11. Revitalising Public Life

1. Dave Lamb, *Mutinies*, London: Solidarity 1978, pp.29-30
2. Hannah Arendt, *The Human Condition*, Chicago: University of Chicago Press, p.53
3. Vic Seidler, 'Fascism and masculinity', *Achilles' Heel*, no. 1, London: Summer 1978, p.21
4. Georgia Sanger, 'The lonely crowd', *Open Road*, no.10, Vancouver: Summer 1979, p.14
5. Luciente, 'The tender trap', *Solidarity*, no.10, London: October-November 1979, p.8
6. Karl Marx and Frederick Engels, *The German Ideology*, in *Karl Marx and Frederick Engels — Collected Works, vol.5*, London: Lawrence & Wishart 1976, pp.229-30
7. Erving Goffman, *The Presentation of Self in Everyday Life*, Harmondsworth: Penguin 1971, pp.118-21, 169

Index

Also published by Pluto Press

Ann Foreman
Femininity as Alienation

Although Marx and Engels developed a historical
account of the oppression of women, they failed to
analyse the strategic link between women's liberation
and proletarian revolution. It was Freud, the pessimistic
liberal, who provided the stress on sexuality missing
from both radical and revolutionary thought.

There have been many attempts to fuse the marxist
and freudian approaches but as Ann Foreman shows in
her careful exploration of Mitchell, Reich and Marcuse's
writings, they have failed. The existentialist approach has
been more productive but it too has provided no basis
for women's liberation.

Ann Foreman argues that the decisive intellectual step
needed now is to establish the centrality of women's
oppression to the organisation of the work process to
capitalism and the exclusion of workers from control
over the means of production. Such a step would
provide the basis for re-stating the terms under which
women's liberation is possible and for exploring the
strategies required for its realisation.

Eli Zaretsky
Capitalism, the Family, and Personal Life

The oppression of women rests on an artificial
distinction between work and personal life which
capitalism creates and constantly reinforces. Eli Zaretsky
shows how the distinction divides the sexes and shapes
the sense of personal identity.

    Zaretsky also shows how the split affected the
socialist movement in the nineteenth century, how it was
reflected in the Russian and Chinese revolutions and is
now reasserting itself in the debate between radical
feminists and traditional socialists.

'an interesting book... thought-provoking for all
students of political science and for a wider, politically
concerned audience.'

Juliet Mitchell.